MEMOIRS

A Rusty Old Halo

ISBN: 978-1-946598-13-4

Truth Book Publishers
www.truthbookpublisher.com

First Printing 2019

ACKNOWLEDGEMENTS

With special appreciation to my wife, Gloria, and my daughter, Anne-Marie, for taking time to edit my manuscript and to give helpful advice.

"A great read and great history lesson."
Rex Walker, CEO, Sombrero Inc. President, North American Boxing Federation

" A captivating read! You can see the hand of God working in a well-lived life, in spite of, the failures and successes."
Dr. Jan King, Retired Professor, Samford University, Birmingham, Alabama

"Put this book on your must read! This is truly a great read, as you follow Joe Turman through his early days, his time in the Marines and his harrowing experiences in Vietnam."
Richard Sherman, Movie Script Writer, Security Chief, Huntsville, Alabama

"This is a delightful read that shows how God took a tough Marine and led him to become a tough missionary in war-torn Vietnam.
Warren Jones, Engineer, Mission Adventurer, Indian Springs, Alabama

"You will find yourself lost in this riveting story, as the author takes you on a long, adventurous journey. Truly a great book for young and old."
Gayle Smith, Re

Table of Contents

MEMOIRS

A Rusty Old Halo

JOE GARNER TURMAN

Early Years

I stood in front of the church after delivering a mission message. A lady walked up and took my hand and said, "If anyone deserves a bright, shiny halo in heaven, it's you foreign missionaries."

I said, "Thank you, but I'll be happy with a rusty old halo."

I thought about my life and how God's hand was on it:

When I was four years-old, I became very sick and almost died. My fever-hot body was lowered into a tub of cold water. Our family doctor, Dr. Walker, said that he had to get the 103 and 104 temperature down, if I was going to make it. My older brother, Gene, and I both had a case of pneumonia. Dr. Walker told some of the folks at the nearby country store that he didn't think I would live through the night. At that time, penicillin had not become available.

My fever did come down, and I bounced back from a near-death experience. God, in His mercy and grace, spared me for a purpose in life.

Since I became spoiled and pampered because of my sickness, I became a demanding terror. Not only did I want my way, I somewhere picked up curse words from the older boys who often hung out at our house. Mama and Papa were chagrined about my cursing, but my older brothers thought it was sorta funny. A neighbor boy warned me that I was going to hell, if I didn't stop my cursing.

Even though I was only four years of age, I knew my profane language was not right. The warning by the neighbor's boy worried me, especially during the night. One night I thought I saw the devil coming after me, and I woke up the household with my screams. After that my cursing diminished considerably.

I grew up in a large family of nine boys and two girls, so there was nothing boring about my childhood. Farm life meant that each of us had some specific chores to carry out. At four years of age, I had the chore of bringing in the kindling for the fireplace. Later, I was given more responsible chores, like feeding the chickens and gathering the eggs.

During cotton picking season, I was anxious to join my older brothers and the hired workers out in the field. Mama gave me a flour sack, and I joined the cotton pickers in the field.

Several families took their children with them to the field. Those three and below were put on blankets under the nearest shade tree. The children, like myself, roamed around in the field. One boy and I ran races. He was fast, but I was just as fast, if not faster. We entertained the cotton pickers with our racing.

When I did get around to picking cotton, I proudly took my flour sack full of cotton to the scales with the others to be weighed. After ceremoniously weighing my sack, my dad said, "Jody boy, you're a good cotton picker. Someday you'll have a large sack like the others."

My brother Bud was fourteen months older than I. We were inseparable, as we did our chores and played together. One evening I was holding a stick of firewood for Bud to trim down to kindling, with an ax. The ax slipped off the wood and cut off my left ring fingernail. It hurt, but I didn't cry.

Mama put my finger in a small pan of kerosene and soaked it there for a while. Evidently, it contained curative elements for my finger healed quickly.

When my older brother's friends visited, they wanted to roam around on the farm and play in the woods. Bud and I wanted to follow them. Our brothers didn't want us around. They warned us, "Don't follow us! Go back and help Mom do some things."

One day when our brother's friends visited, we followed them to the swimming hole. We hid in the bushes and watched their swimming hole antics, until they saw us. Our brothers charged into the bushes and grabbed us before we could escape. To the raucous laughter of their friends, they threw us into the swimming hole, clothes and all.

Then, they all disappeared. Neither Bud nor I could swim. We struggled to the surface and seeing no one around to save us, we started paddling. That was our first and only swimming lesson. From that time on, we were swimmers.

To this day, I don't know whether my brothers and friends were hiding in the bushes watching to see if we made it, or not.

Bud and I spent many fun hours playing with our neighbor, Charles Mckinney. We would meet Charles at our mailbox which was located on the corner of the farm and market road and the three-hundred-yard lane going to our house.

Charles was in the same grade as Bud. His younger brother, Carroll, sometimes came along, but he was too young to keep up with our fast moves.

One of our favorite past time was robbing wasp nests. We would each get a branch from a tree and stand in a tight circle in front of the wasp nest. A well- aimed rock would knock the nest down, and out would come the angry wasps. The dive- bombing wasps would try to penetrate the swinging tree branches. Sometimes a wasp would get through and sting one of us.

My Uncle Tood came and spent a month or more with us each summer. He owned a large restaurant in Dallas, but he had to sell it, after he suffered a stroke that left him paralyzed on one side. He loved to come and spend time with our family, and with his younger sister, my Mom.

Uncle Tood slept in every morning and got up long after Papa and my older brothers were working in the fields. Mom prepared his favorite breakfast foods. After breakfast, Uncle Tood walked into the woods and hunted for guinea eggs. Mom had a large flock of chickens, and thirty guineas stressed up their lives.

The guineas slept in trees near the barn. They were cantankerous fowls who lived on the edge of a domestic life-style. They screeched and made unearthly sounds that intimidated the chickens. They often ran the chickens off and gobbled up their food.

On the positive side, they didn't require much up-keep since they spent most of their time in the woods. At night, they gave a screeching warning, if any person or animal came near the house or barn. They foraged for their own food and stayed away all day. While in the woods, they laid their eggs in the most secret place they could find.

Now, this is why Uncle Tood and I enjoyed the sport of finding guinea eggs in the woods. It was a challenge, and we dedicated several hours each morning to search for guinea eggs. When we came near a nest of eggs, the hen would leave the nest and leave the vicinity. The hens were smart enough to know that, if we could see them, then we could be diverted from seeing the nest.

Not only did Uncle Tood enjoy finding guinea eggs, he enjoyed eating them. The eggs were smaller than chicken eggs, so Mom would cook him six eggs in the morning.

Billy and Tony, were our neighbors, lived about a quarter of a mile from us. One evening on Christmas Eve, we were all sitting around the fire place enjoying a roaring hearth-warming fire from the big back logs, when suddenly we were startled out of our wits by loud, sharp explosions.

Billy and Tony had sneaked up to our house and had thrown large firecrackers on our front porch. My older brothers charged outside, and soon we could hear them laughing together with Tony and Billy. The boys all came in to drink punch and eat a piece of Mama Turman's chocolate cake.

Every Christmas, we younger children hung our stockings on the fireplace for Santa to fill with goodies. We didn't get all the things that we wanted, but Mama made sure that we received some of the things we requested Santa to bring us.

My free years came to an end, when I entered the first grade of school.

School years

Like most six-year-olds I was excited about starting to school. Mrs. Twain, a tall, slim lady, taught the first grade. Although patient and kind, she could apply the paddle when she needed to. On one occasion, she paddled me and then hugged me with tears in her eyes.

Mrs. Twain's husband served overseas in the Army. One day, at recess, when I came back into the classroom to get something, I saw Mrs. Twain with her head down on the desk, crying. I felt sad in my heart for her and tip toed out of the room.

Noonday School was the typical rough country school, of that time. Each boy would be tested for his wrestling and fisticuff abilities. On a cold November morning, before classes started, I stood near the pot-bellied stove in the first-grade room trying to keep warm. My older brother Pat, and his classmate, Jaybo, came into the classroom. Pat said to me, "Come on out and wrestle Larry Neely."

I dutifully took off my coat and followed them outside, where Larry was waiting for me.

Larry was a stocky-built first grader. We wrestled to a draw before a crowd of cheering boys. Later on in life, Larry and I became the only two from the Noonday School era who were ordained as ministers of the Gospel.

Later, I wrestled Donald during recess. All though Donald was in my class, he was a year and half older and much larger. He wrestled me down, and I fell on my left arm and broke it. It hurt like crazy. The principal took me home, and Papa took me to the doctor.

The doctor put my arm in a cast, and I stayed out of school for several days. When I returned to my class, I felt something like a wounded war hero. The teacher and my classmates all gave me special attention. My classmates wanted to sign my cast.

During early spring when I was in the second grade, I stayed home from school with a bad cold and fever. In the middle of the day, Billy, our fifteen-year-old neighbor, came running up to the house screaming and crying. I looked out the window to see Papa run across the field with him to a clump of trees.

About an hour later, I saw a number of people gathered near the clump of trees. After a while, six men emerged from the trees each gripping the corner of a white sheet. Mama saw me watching. She said, "Billy's dad has had an accident and he's dead."

Mama was trying to protect me from some harsh realities of life. Later, as I grew older, I learned that Billy's dad had committed suicide.

Soon after the tragedy, Billy and Tony moved away. We missed them. Even to this day, we still remember Billy and Tony.

War Years and Beyond

During that time of my life, I remember Pearl Harbor and its effect on our community and lives. Our neighbor died, as a result of a car accident, two days before Pearl Harbor. It was a dark, overcast and gloomy day, and the news of Pearl Harbor and our neighbor's death, made the day seem even sadder and darker.

Mama and Papa left to go to our neighbor's funeral. I didn't want them to leave the house. All of the devastating news made me feel insecure, and I wanted the family to stay close together.

.Many of the young men in Noonday volunteered to serve in the Armed Forces. When they walked past the school yard in their uniforms, we watched them with admiration. The older boys called out words of encouragement to them.

At school we were marched into a darkened room to watch Victory Films. We gave our dimes for victory bonds and wished that we could go and fight the "Nips' and "Krauts."

Dan, my oldest brother, worked in the CC Camps. After Pearl Harbor, Dan came home bringing Clifford Miller with him, for they had become friends at the CC Camp. Cliff, a red-headed, fun-loving Irishman, kept our household in stitches. He told one story, or joke, after another. He called Mama "Mother Turman" and told her dozens of times how much he liked her cooking. We knew he was sincere, because he ate each meal like it was his last meal.

After a week at home, Dan and Cliff joined the army and left for basic training. After three months in the army, Dan received a medical discharge because of his hay fever. The doctors said that he would not last a day amid all the dust and spray of a mobile Army.

One afternoon in late August, as we were sitting on the back porch, we saw someone coming down the country gravel road carrying a duffle bag on his shoulder. Dan's dog, Boy, who was part police and part collie, stood up from where he was laying in the yard. He sniffed the air and stood erect for a few seconds, then he shot across the yard like a bullet, and raced toward the coming distant figure. Mama stood up and cried out, "It's Danny boy!"

We still couldn't see who it was, but we all knew that it had to be Dan; and it was Dan. We all got up and raced down the road to greet him.

Dan never really got over his early discharge from the army. Although he came back home, got a job and married a very nice lady, he felt like he had been left behind. Clifford, on the other hand, fought through the battles of Italy and France and later was killed in a jeep accident in Germany.

My older brothers, Charlie and Gene, joined the Marines, as soon as they were old enough to volunteer. Charlie's battalion was in training to take Japan's mainland, when atomic bombs were dropped on Hiroshima and Nagasaki. Charlie served for a year with the occupational forces in Japan. Gene served stateside with the security forces.

We younger boys worked with Papa on the farm raising cotton, corn, tomatoes and other garden vegetables. While working in the fields during the summertime, we learned to spot and name the different kinds of aircraft flying over the Texas sky. Texas had many air fields, so the skies were often full of military planes.

Our neighbor, Martin Thetford, joined the Army Air Corp. Martin buzzed our house and fields where we were working several times. One time he came in so low, that we could see him wave at us.

Late one afternoon, we were sitting on the back porch listening to the war news on the radio. It was D-Day, and we were all concerned about our soldiers over there. Thunder storms had rolled through the countryside earlier in the day. Now huge white clouds crowded the eastern skyline just before sunset. We all sat quietly watching the sky enjoying the evening breeze. Bud suddenly shouted, “Look at the V in the clouds!”

It was there. The clouds formed a distinct V just above the horizon. Mama said, “That’s a sign for us. Our boys are going to win the battle and the war.”

A number of other people in Noonday saw the V sign that evening. We interpreted it as a sign from the Lord that Allied Forces would be victorious in the war.

When Charlie and Gene returned home, we could see the change in them. They were larger, more muscled, handsome, sun-tanned and they also had a new worldview. They had seen other states, countries and cultures. They had passed movie stars on the streets of Hollywood and had tasted the exciting life-style of another world, so radically different from rural Noonday, that they would never be content to live in the slow-moving community again.

Meanwhile, back on the farm, we younger children had grown up and assumed more responsibilities on the farm.

One Saturday, during the middle of summer, Bud and I walked to our friend’s house not far from the Neches

River. After playing around his house for a while, we decided to go for a swim in the Big Eddy, which was the widest part of the river. To swim across the Big Eddy was a challenge for a eleven and twelve-year-old. Even though we grew tired during the last twenty yards, we made it okay.

After our swim, we played in the nearby woods. Then we heard a lot of yelling and commotion down at the river bank; so we ran down to see what was happening. Three men had just pulled a man, and his six-year-old son out of the river.

The man had tried to swim across the Big Eddy with his son on his back. Twenty yards from the river bank he gave out and tried to get his son off his back. The son panicked and hugged him around the neck so tight that he cut off his breath. They both drowned. For months afterwards, I could see that man and his son lying dead on the river bank, their faces discolored by the death of drowning.

Every summer when the crops were laid by, we had our mid-summer revival. During the time of revival, we worked in the fields until four o'clock. We boys left a bar of soap at the swimming hole, so we could bathe quickly. Then we could do our chores and get ready for the revival meeting.

The church was packed out every night during revival. Whether Methodist or Baptist, almost everyone in the community attended the meetings. Attending revival was a time for spiritual renewal, and also a social event. Noonday was a farming community, and most people worked hard and seldom visited during the summer season.

Grand Ole Opry

One day in the middle of June, Papa assigned us boys the task of chopping the cotton in the south cotton patch. Before he left us with our work, he turned and said, "Boys, if you knock out this cotton patch today, tonight we'll go to the Tyler Fair Grounds and hear Roy Acuff and the Smokey Mountain Boys.

Papa knew how to motivate us. We picked up our hoes and worked like Trojans. By four o'clock we had finished chopping the cotton. We felt good about our accomplishment.

Chopping cotton means to chop around each individual cotton stalk with your hoe so that you clean out all the grass or weeds around the plant. Then the plant's growth will not be hindered.

After finishing our assignment, we raced down to the swimming hole and plunged in and took our bath. Refreshed, we went to the barn and did our chores. Then we gulped down our supper and slipped on clean shirts and jeans. Papa started the truck and we all piled in; the older boys sat in the cab with Papa, and we younger boys sat in the truck bed.

When we arrived at the Fair Grounds, all the tickets had been sold out. Disappointed is not the word; we felt frustrated and tired as we walked back toward our truck. On the way to our truck, we met Roy Acuff himself. He had on his cover-all, he had been out doing some work on the equipment, while the light weights warmed up the crowd.

Roy stopped and asked Papa, "Where are you all going? You're going the wrong way."

Papa said, "Roy, we're glad to have you down here in Texas. We came to hear you, but the tickets are all sold out. I promised these boys that we'd hear you all tonight. We're all disappointed."

Roy Acuff looked bigger than life to me. Every Saturday night we listened to the Grand Ole Opry out of Ryman Auditorium in Nashville and heard Roy sing. As a ten-year-old boy, I could hardly believe I was looking at the great Roy Acuff. His hair was jet black and wavy. His black eyes matched his hair. He looked down and smiled at us boys and showed his pearly white teeth. He was a handsome man.

Something must have moved in Roy's heart for he said, "You'll come with me. I'll get you some seats."

He took us in and got us some of the best seats near the stage.

In 1989, my family and I were on a furlough from the mission field in Indonesia. I was to speak at a church in Nashville. On Saturday morning, the pastor told us, if we wanted to see the Grand Ole Opry, he could get us some backstage seats. We were excited about that.

While sitting back stage before the show, I asked a stage hand, "Can we visit the Opry Stars in their dressing rooms?"

The stage hand said, "If the stage door is open, you can."

I asked him, "Is Roy Acuff here tonight?"

The stage hand said, "Yeah, he's here. He's getting up in the years, but he's usually here and will be singing later on. If his stage door is open, it means you can go in and visit."

Roy Acuff's door was open, and I saw him sitting facing the door. After introducing myself, I told him the story that happened in 1944, at Tyler, Texas.

I added, "Roy, I want to thank you for your kind act. My family has never forgotten you. You're still one of our favorites."

Roy laughed and said, "I'm glad you shared that with me. I can't remember that happening, because you know I've been in so many places. Thanks for dropping by. You've made my day."

We were in Africa in 1993, when we heard the news that Roy Acuff had passed away. I could visualize the dark, dancing eyes and quick smile. We were saddened by the news.

Attending School During the War Years

During the war years, most all of our teachers at Noonday Elementary School were women. We boys were a rough, rugged, and rowdy bunch, and the women teachers couldn't handle us. We often brought our sling-shots to school and had warfare shooting green plums, at one another. It's a wonder that someone didn't lose an eye.

We found a way to get into the gymnasium through a back window. The gym was kept closed, except during basketball season and special events. During recess we often disappeared from the schoolyard and hid in the gym. The girls and teachers searched for us but couldn't find us. When we were satisfied that they had given up, we suddenly appeared on the school yard.

Mrs. Murphy, the principal asked, "Where were you boys?"

With innocent looks, "Oh, we were just playing around the back of the school yard."

Mrs. Murphy and the other teachers never had a clue about our disappearance.

Mrs. Wilson was my sixth grade teacher. She was a tall, heavy-set lady who was very sensitive about her size and weight. She would lay into us boys with her large paddle and beat the fire out of us. She seemed to feel that all of us boys were incorrigible and always up to no good (She was right). She would whip us at the slightest provocation.

My brother, Bud, was in Mrs. Murphy's class. He was her star pupil and graduated at the head of the class. However, Bud felt that Mrs. Wilson was not handling the boys in her class in a just manner, so he decided to tease her. He came to school early one morning and went into my classroom and drew an uncomplimentary picture of Mrs. Wilson on the blackboard. He drew her as a woman weighing about three hundred pounds.

When Mrs. Wilson arrived at school and went into her classroom, she was infuriated. She kept us boys in at recess and asked us who drew the picture. None of us knew who did it, and even if we did, we would not have told her. Finally, she dismissed us.

The following days, Mrs. Wilson locked the classroom door. The next week Bud discovered a transom (an air hole) behind the large pot-bellied stove. It was large enough for him to crawl through. He found out that he could go to the crawl space under the school, and crawl up to the air hole into the Mrs. Wilson's room.

Bud came to school early one morning and crawled into Mrs. Wilson's classroom and drew another picture of her on the blackboard. When she came into her classroom and saw the picture, she was steaming mad. She told us boys that she was keeping us after school, and she intended to find out who did the drawing. We all foresaw a whipping coming.

Actually, we boys didn't know who drew the picture. We suspected who did it, but we wouldn't tell her. We encouraged one another to take our whipping and not cry.

After school, Mrs. Wilson interrogated us to try to get someone to confess to the crime. She said, "If the one who did it will confess, then I won't whip everybody. But if no one confesses, I'm going to whip every one of you. Now, who did it?"

She towered over us and stormed, "I said who did it?"

During the time of our interrogation, Bud had crawled back under the schoolhouse and listened to the proceeding at the air hole behind the stove. He could not resist answering the second demanding question, "Who did it?" He shouted out through the air hole, "I did, I did!"

His voice ricocheted around the room and bounced off the walls. We were just as surprised as Mrs. Wilson. She shouted out, "Who said that? Who said that? Which one of you said that?"

After all of us refused to say anything, Mrs. Wilson said, "Line up in the hallway and come in one at a time for your whipping"

While waiting for our turn, we could hear the loud whack, whack of the paddle on our classmate's rears. We listened to see if anyone cried. No one cried.

Mrs. Wilson never knew that Bud was the culprit who drew the pictures. Bud never told anyone in the school that he did it. He didn't even tell me, but I knew that he was the one. Bud graduated with honors and went on to attend the Tyler Middle and high schools.

Many things changed when Mr. Burns came to be the principal of Noonday School. He was a short, stocky-built man in his early fifties. He had taught school for many years and knew how to handle students, especially boys.

On the first day of school, the bell rang for recess. Curtis Casey did his regular exit out the window to beat everyone else to the playground. Mr. Burns called him back into the room. He instructed Curtis, "Now, I want you to jump out the window and run back into the room here and do it again until I tell you to stop."

When Curtis jumped on the window sill and planted his feet to jump out the window, Mr. Burns whacked him on the rear with his broad paddle. Curtis made his round and came back, jumped on the window sill, whack! After five rounds Curtis' tongue was hanging out and his rear was burning. He went two more rounds before Mr. Burns told him to stop.

Curtis never jumped out the window again. After witnessing that scene, none of us dared to jump out the window.

Mr. Burns organized us boys into basketball and soft ball teams. We were rough and rowdy, but we could play sports. Our basketball team seldom lost a game. Mr. Burns, not only was a good teacher, he was a good coach.

Under Mr. Burns' leadership I enjoyed my seventh and eight-grade classes and school sports.

When we were out for recess one day, I returned to my classroom to get a baseball glove. I noticed that Mr. Burns was still sitting behind his desk. He looked sad. I later learned that his son, Johnny Frank, had died in an airplane crash while training to go overseas, and Mr. Burns had just received the news.

Making the Football Team

After graduating from the eighth grade at Noonday, I went to Hogg Junior High School in Tyler. I wanted to go out for football, but I knew that Papa would not give his consent. Papa didn't know anything about football, and he thought it was a crazy game that didn't make sense. Baseball and boxing were the only sports that Papa had any use for.

When I faced up to the fact that Papa would never give me permission to play football, I began to talk to Mama about my dream of playing football. I told her, "Mama, you know I can run fast, and I can make the team. This is something I really want to do."

While Mama cooked supper for us, she listened to my request. After a few minutes, she said, "I'll talk to your dad about it. You know, I think you'll make a good football player."

Two days before school started, Mama came up to me with a smile on her face. "Jody boy, Papa said you can play football."

I wasn't prone to show affection, but I hugged Mama; however, I knew it was going to be a challenge. I didn't know anyone on the team and had never played anything, except touch football.

Andy Woods was the coach for Hogg Junior High School. He knew boys and how to challenge them to do their best on and off the field. The first day of practice, he had us run a fifty yard race. I came in second behind Clarence Mooney. Clarence was a natural runner and the fastest ninth grader that I've ever seen.

Next, Coach Woods had us line up to catch passes. I had played a lot of touch football at Noonday, and I could catch passes. I hardly ever dropped one. Coach Woods pointed me out to the other players: "Look, this guy never drops the ball. He's got glue on his hands."

That compliment encouraged me. We ran the single wing formation, and I ran first string wing back on the team. I also played corner back on defense.

We had a winning team, and I shared my position with another ninth grader. On the final game of the season we played Roberts Junior High School, which was on the other side of Tyler. The boys who played for Roberts were mostly from blue-collar working families, like me. They had a good team.

The Hogg-Roberts game was the big game for both teams, and the Tyler paper gave it good publicity. Coach Woods told me that I was going to start the game. I didn't know it until later on that I was mentioned in the write-up as one of the main running stars for the Hogg team. That surprised me.

I didn't make any touchdowns in the game, but I did make some good runs. Clarence Mooney was put in to run special plays. Once he got a step on the defense, he was gone. He did get a step on the Roberts defenders and raced sixty yards for a touchdown.

Clarence didn't really like football. He was a track star, and he probably could have run in the Olympics had he pursued his track career.

My time at middle school came to an end, and I looked toward becoming a sophomore in high school.

High School Days

Often, going from middle school to high school can be traumatic, exciting, apprehensive and challenging for a teenager. Although I wanted to play football, I thought I was too small; instead, I went out for basketball.

I weighed 135 pounds, but I was fast. The coach placed me on the B team, but he gave very little time to coaching the B team. He assigned some running and passing drills and let us do our own thing. Needless to say, I learned nothing new about how to play basketball.

After several weeks working out with the B team, I quit basketball. First of all, I was bored with it, and secondly, I had to hitch-hike home every afternoon after practice. Some afternoons I couldn't catch a ride, so I had to spend the night with my brother Dan, and his family.

I think the straw that broke the camel's back was the afternoon when I caught a ride, and the man let me out on the highway several miles from my house. Since it was beginning to rain, I decided to take a short-cut through the woods. While I was in the middle of the woods, a rain storm suddenly blew up. It turned pitch dark in a matter of minutes. I couldn't see my hands, when I held them in front of my face.

Even though it was pitch dark, I kept moving through the driving rain of a cool autumn downpour. Soaked by the rain, I kept moving to keep warm. I didn't know and couldn't see where I was going. I ran into a shallow creek, briar bushes, trees and fell into a three-foot ditch. Scratched and bleeding, I kept trying to find my way out of the forest of trees, but I could not. I kept going in a circle, because I was disoriented.

Finally, the rain storm blew over and the heavy black clouds rolled by, and I could see a welcome star above me. Then I could see just enough to find my way out of the woods.

When I arrived home, Mama had a warm supper waiting for me. She said, "You're later than usual, Jody boy."

I was embarrassed about getting lost in the woods, so I casually said, "The rain sorta slowed me down."

I found some iodine and put it on my scratches. Not only did I not want to mention getting lost in the woods, I didn't want to worry Mama about my scratched up arms and legs.

The next day I decided that basketball was not worth the trouble of trying to find a ride home every afternoon after practice. I told the coach that I was quitting basketball. He just nodded okay. Really, he didn't know me and didn't care if I stayed, or not.

Later on in January, I played for my homeroom basketball team in the school tournament. Our homeroom team went all the way to the finals. Our homeroom voted to name our team the "Turman Terrors."

Playing Varsity Football

I went out for football in my junior year. When we ran the sprints, I usually came in first or second. This caught the coach's eye. He asked me, "Why didn't you come out last year?'

"I was too small, coach."

"Baloney, if you can run fast, you're not too small. You should've come out."

Since I was new on the team, I started playing on the B team. In the first game, I sprinted for a forty-yard touchdown. The coach told me, "Turman, I'm going to use you in the varsity game at Highland Park. Learn your plays and be ready."

I did learn my plays, and I tingled with excitement about the possibility of playing against the Highland Park Scotties in Dallas. During the meeting in the locker room, just before we went out on the field, Coach Henig suddenly asked me, "Turman, what do you do on forty-two?"

I knew the play, but the excitement of the moment and being put on the spot caused my heart to pound and my throat to constrict. Several seconds ticked by, and before I could blurt out the answer, Coach Henig said, "Turman, you've gotta learn your plays if you're gonna play."

The coach did not put me in that night. I was ready to play, and I felt like I could have run for a touchdown. But alas, my opportunity to play had slipped by in a moment of time, and I was not given an opportunity to show what I could do on the field.

That year, my junior year, I was voted the Class Favorite. I don't know why, because I was bashful and did not participate in any school social activities. Invitations came to participate in different dances and activities, but I ignored all of them. I had no car and did not have the financial means to have a date and attend these functions.

Tyler High School was a large Texas school whose students came from all classes of society. Students from rich families, as well as poor families, composed the student body. We students really didn't pay much attention to rich or poor backgrounds. The one thing that separated poor students from richer ones was that the students from wealthy families had cars.

During spring practice, I nailed down first team running back position. I was the right half-back on the split-T formation. I liked the formation and how quick you can get through the hole in the line and be in the secondary. If the secondary was out of position, or was blocked, you could score.

In July, we heard that Coach Henig had resigned, and we would have a new coach. When we reported for practice in late August, our new coach told us that we would run from a single-wing formation. I ran from the wing-back position. Lining up behind the wide-receiver, I blocked, went out for passes and ran reverses two or three times during a game.

I didn't like the new formation for several reasons. First of all, we didn't have a good passing game. Secondly, I would only get to run the ball two or three times in a game, and most of my running would be east and west before I could cut it up the field.

I played offense and defense. On defense I played cornerback. In a game during the last week in October, a cold Texas northerner blew up and dropped the temperatures below freezing. It was cold that night, and we had a sparse crowd. *If I wasn't playing, I wouldn't be here as a fan.*

In the last quarter of the game, a wide receiver did a post route, caught the ball, eluded the safety and headed for the goal. I raced after him from my position. At the ten yard line, I realized that I could not catch him from behind, even though I had gained on him, so I took a flying leap at his heels in an effort to trip him. His shoe cleats came down on my hand on the frozen turf. My hand hurt, but I finished the game.

Saturday and Sunday my hand swelled, turned black and hurt. Finally, on late Sunday afternoon, I told Papa and Mama that I thought my hand was broken. Monday morning Papa took me to our family doctor, and he confirmed that my hand was broken. He said, "Your football season is over. Your hand needs to be in a cast for a month or more."

Needless to say, I was disappointed that I would not finish the season. The following week, the team had a bye (a week off). The next game was in Wichita Falls. I accompanied the team and sat in the broadcast booth as a spotter for the announcer.

In the bye week, Coach Prejean came back to the T-formation. I felt a tinge of resentment, because I felt I had been marginalized as a wing back in single-wing formation, and now as soon as I'm out for the season, he put in the T-formation.

Boyd Murphy took my place on the team, and he really shined as he burst through the line and raced forty-five yards for a touchdown at Wichita Falls. I thought, *we should have been running that formation all season.*

The last game of the season was on Thanksgiving afternoon, and I knew the seniors would be recognized. I wanted to attend the game; however, we lived nine miles from Tyler, and I had no way to go to the game. Papa had a truck but he was using it to haul some things.

I felt extremely frustrated and marginalized in life. Several times I started to walk a mile over to the main highway to try to catch a ride to Tyler, but I didn't do it. When I finally made up my mind that I should and could hitch-hike to Tyler, it was already too late. I missed the opportunity of being at the last game. I could only hear it on the radio.

Grinding out the Last Days in High School

My remaining months as a senior at Tyler High School were not pleasant for me. I didn't participate in the spring sports, baseball or track. My classes were a bore, and I could hardly wait to get out of school.

In February, I started working out at Curley Mahan's gym with my brother Bud. After a stint in the Navy, Bud came back to Tyler with a desire to be a boxer. Curley was the best boxer in the area, and he enjoyed teaching teens and young men how to handle themselves in the ring.

After working out a few weeks, Curley lined Bud and I up to fight in a Tuesday night smoker at his club. Bud was to fight Don Holmes, and I was to go against O.J. Helms. O.J. was a junior in high school, and he was the welterweight champ in East Texas. He was tough and all of his brothers were tough. When they climbed into the ring, the Helm brothers won their fights.

On the day of the fight I was in the restroom at school in a stall. Two boys came in and they were discussing the coming fight. One of them said, "Joe Turman is gonna fight O.J. tonight."

"Yeah," said his friend, "O.Js gonna beat his butt off."

When I heard that conversation, it made me fighting mad. *I'll see about that.*

Bud was my second. I climbed into the ring and glanced over toward O.J's corner. He was already there waiting for the fight to start. He looked confident; the bell rang, and I went out to the center of the ring and faced O.J.

I started bobbing and weaving and throwing out a few jabs. I was trying to be clever. O.J. just stood there looking at all my bobbing and weaving, then he threw his right hand and the lick bounced off my forehead and knocked me down.

I was more stunned than hurt. At the count of six, I stood up, and O.J. came in to finish me off. I hit him square on the chin with a right hand and stopped him in his tracks. He had a surprised look on his face. I flicked out a left jab, followed up with a right hand and staggered O.J.

If I had been an experienced boxer, I could have finished off O.J.; but instead of coming in and following up on him, I led with several jabs and moved to his right. The momentum of the fight changed in my favor. We slugged it out for two more rounds, and I won the decision.

Bud also won his fight over Don Holmes that night. I was his second.

The next morning my left hand was swollen. The family doctor took an X-Ray and said it was broken. I would have to wear a cast for six weeks.

Boxing and a victory helped me to bear the rest of the school year. My brother, Bud, went on to become an amateur champion and, later on, a sensational professional heavyweight, known as Buddy Turman.

Finally, graduation day came around. Papa took me to the ceremony in his truck. A large crowd attended the graduation. After the program was over, I walked with Papa back down the street from the high school to the truck. It was late May, and the sun was just going down and lighting up the clouds to form a spectacular sunset. *I'm going to see what's on the other side of that sunset.*

I'm going to see the world. I'm out of here as soon as possible.

Where the Rubber Meets the Road

In due time, I did see more of the world than I could ever imagine. In the meantime, I was offered a job working in a ceramic factory making decent wages. I bought a second-hand Ford car, and I needed to pay for it.

I played baseball for the Noonday Oilers on Sunday afternoons. Everything seemed to be going along well for me, but this was coming to an end.

It had been a hot day in the middle of June. After work, I longed for a cool swim. Putting on my bathing suit, I headed for the swimming hole, which was located on the family farm, almost a mile from the house.

Walking along, I thought about the baseball game that I had played the previous Sunday. We played semi-pro teams from other communities around us. I went over some of the plays in my mind. Two times I had bobbled the ball at shortstop and failed to get the batters out at first. Once I had struck out at bat, but I had hit three singles.

Being the youngest player on the team, I took a lot of kidding. After I hit a grounder and failed to beat the throw to first base, my older team mates hollered, "Grandma was slow, but she was old." After I fumbled the ball at shortstop, the first baseman shouted, "Com'm on Joe, take a pill."

I didn't mind their kidding at all. Most of them were World War 11 veterans who had fought in France, Germany and stormed the beaches in the Pacific. I felt honored to play with them. I had just turned eighteen.

The trail to the swimming hole was so familiar that I could walk it on auto pilot. I didn't need to think where I was going. While walking along with my mind on the past baseball game, I felt a sharp pain in my lower right ankle. Thinking that I had stepped on a thorn, I reached down to pull it out. Then I saw the coiled ground rattlesnake getting ready to strike again.

I quickly moved away and looked for a rock to kill the snake; however, I couldn't find a rock, a stick or anything to kill the snake. He slithered away. My ankle hurt like crazy. Our neighbors, the McKays, lived at the edge of our farm near the highway. I walked over to their house to get some help; however, no one was at home.

Since their front door was unlocked, I went into their bathroom, found a razor blade and cut an X over the snakebite; then I tied a piece of cloth above the bite on my lower leg. Hobbling out to the highway, I tried to thumb a ride to Tyler to get medical help. No car would stop for me. I wasn't surprised, for a young man in a bathing suit with a baseball cap on, and a bandage on his leg trying to flag down a ride, presents a doubtful figure.

Finally, a man driving an old truck picked me up and took me to a clinic on South Broadway in Tyler. My leg had already began to swell. They gave me an anti-venom shot and told me they wanted to keep me overnight.

I asked to use a phone to call Mama and Papa. Mama and Papa didn't know what had happened to me, and they were worried. After telling them about the snake bite, I said, "I didn't want to walk all the way back to the house, so I went out to the highway and caught a ride to town. I'm okay, but they want to keep me overnight."

Papa said, "I'll come up and get you in the morning."

I missed work that day, because I still had some swelling in my lower leg. When I came back to work the following day, the boss told me that I was fired. I explained to him that a snake had bitten me, and I couldn't come to work. He thought I was making up a story and wouldn't consider taking me back.

Jobs were scarce, and now I was out of work.

Working on the Railroad

After I lost my job at the ceramic factory, I got together with old buddies from Noonday and Tyler to go look for work in Ft. Worth. Before we nailed down a place to stay, we went to the employment office to find work. The man who interviewed us knew how to handle tough young men.

He said to us, "I've got a construction job for all of you, but I doubt if you're tough enough to handle it. All of the young men who've come through here, so far, have all quit after one or two days."

He challenged us, so we said, "We can do it, and we won't quit."

He smiled and said, "I hope I don't see you all back in here next week."

We all answered in chorus, "Don't worry. You won't see our faces again."

From the employment office, we found inexpensive rooms down in the shabbiest part of Ft. Worth. Not only was the neighborhood shabby, it was a mean area.

The next morning we reported to the construction office for work. The man in the office drew us a map on how to get to the construction site. We all piled into one car and drove to the site which was located about fifteen miles west of Ft. Worth, not far from Granbury. The work consisted of tearing out an old railroad track.

The work was difficult, because the old rails had to be pried loose from the railroad ties and loaded on a truck. All of the loose spikes and other pieces of iron had to be cleaned up and loaded on a vehicle. It was back-breaking work, and after two days on the job, we could see why a number of people had quit the job.

A man that everyone called Pop drove one of the trucks. He was the foreman's father-in-law. We liked to tease Pop. When we found out that he was from Pittsburg, we told him that the state anthem was "There's A Pawnshop on the Corner in Pittsburg, Pennsylvania." After that, every time Pop drove up for us to load the truck, we sang this song and Pop would get angry…red-in-the-face angry.

We worked six days a week, ten hours a day, and Sunday was the only day we had off. We didn't get paid until after the second week on the job. By that time, our money had run out and we were on a starvation diet. We took a peanut butter sandwich to work with us, and when we had a few moments to lean on our crow bars, we would mention our favorite foods.

There was a consensus among us about the kind of food we wanted when we got paid. We all wanted a good steak, and we wanted to get it at the Cattleman's Steak House in downtown Ft. Worth.

The glorious day came when we got paid. We pocketed our pay and headed for Cattleman's Steak House to make our dreams a reality. We all ordered a big steak. Was it ever good! When we finished, we were still hungry, so we called the waitress over and ordered another steak. She said, "Are you kidding me? I can't believe you want another steak."

We answered, "Believe us because we've been starving for the past two weeks."

The waitress laughed so hard that she dropped the silverware that she had in her hands.

Although it was good, it was difficult finishing the second steak. We walked out of the steak house with our stomachs pouching out like overfed puppies.

There was a lot of theft that took place in our neighborhood. A tall` six-foot four bachelor lived down the street from us. He drove a nice car and kept it parked as close to his rented room as possible. One night someone stole his hub caps, and for some reason, he thought we did it.

It was Sunday night, and we were already in bed, after a busy day of going about town on our day off. At around ten o'clock, we were abruptly awakened by someone kicking in our door and shouting, "I know you did it. Give me my hub caps back, or I'm going to come in and clean up on all of you."

I stood up in bed with the hairs standing up on the back of my neck. Whatever else, I didn't want that big bruiser coming in on us. I grabbed a pair of binoculars on the lamp table, beside the bed, and pointed them like a pistol. I shouted out with all the macho that I could muster, "If you come in, someone will carry you out."

My bluff worked for the man couldn't see whether I had a pistol, or not, in our dark bedroom. He backed up a half-step and muttered something. I said to him, "We didn't take your hub caps. We don't know anything about them. Besides, they don't fit our car. You've got the wrong people."

The man backed up another step. "Somebody took 'em, and I heard it was you all. I'm gonna find out who did it."

The first week in September, the construction company finished its job tearing up the old railroad tracks. The boss came to us and said, "Our next job is in Kansas. You boys are good workers. Come on to Kansas with us."

We thanked him for the invite but declined. Kansas seemed so far away, and the construction work was very hard. We had had enough for a while.

After the construction job, Bub Tomlinson and I got a job in Ft. Worth working for an aircraft company as apprentice machinists. One day, for no apparent reason, the boss over our section called us in and said, "I'm going to terminate you."

We just looked at him as the word "terminate" rolled around in our minds. We were trying to get a handle on what he was saying to us. Seeing the puzzled look on our faces, he said, "You're fired. We don't need you anymore. You haven't been in the military."

That was it. We had tried to get jobs in several places, but were turned down because we were of the age to be drafted into the military services.

Boarding House Battle

In a transition state, trying to find out what I wanted to do, I returned to Noonday and Tyler, Texas, to try to find out what I wanted to do next. I had in mind that I wanted to join the US Marines. Since it was November, I would wait until after Thanksgiving and Christmas before I joined up.

My high school friend, Don, and I were hanging out together at that time. One day, we ate at a popular boarding house that was known for its tasty home-cooked noon meals. After I ate, I started to leave the table, not knowing that I was supposed to take my plate to the kitchen.

One of the young men who worked at the boarding house, stopped me, and said in a commanding voice, "Hey you! Get your plate and take it to the kitchen."

He spoke in such a belligerent voice that it made me angry. I said, "You take it back yourself, if you want it in the kitchen."

"You come outside with me," he said.

When he said that, I interpreted it as a challenge to duel with our fists, like meet me at high noon on Main Street. I followed the young man outside, along with my friend, Don, and four of the young man's friends.

When we came out to the yard, the young man turned and said, "Okay, this is far enough." When he turned to face me, I slugged him right on the nose. Blood spurted out and he danced about the yard holding his nose and moaning, "Oh, oh, aw, it hurts."

He put a handkerchief over his nose and walked over to his friends. They looked toward us, but then turned and walked back into the house.

Don said, "Let's get outta here before more trouble comes."

The next day, the owners of the boarding house reported me to the Sheriff, saying that I assaulted the young man. The Sheriff called Papa and asked him about the incident. Papa said to me, "What happened Jody boy?"

I explained what had taken place. Papa called the Sheriff and told him what I said. I heard him say to the Sheriff, "You know how young men are. If they're challenged like that, they'll fight. My son just got in the first lick."

The Sheriff told Papa. "You're right, Floyd. Tell your son to stay away from that boarding house, okay?"

I never did meet the young man again. He probably made a fine citizen and family man. Hopefully, his public relations improved.

On to the Marines

In early January, I joined the marines. I asked some of my old football buddies, Bobby Rogers, Don Socia and Joe Palmer to join with me. We went down to the recruiting office and talked with the Sergeant. He was happy to see us and was more than willing to sign us up. He said, "Get down here at eight tomorrow morning to get on the bus to Dallas. At Dallas you'll get a physical and be sworn in.

The next morning we were at the recruiting office on time. Joe Palmer and Don Socia thought it over and changed their minds. They said, "Hey, we want to join the army. Our dad and brothers were all army, so we're going to stick with the army."

Only Bobby Rogers and I boarded the bus for Dallas. The large recruiting depot in Dallas was full of young men who were going into all the different branches of service. When they called for the Marine volunteers to come for our physicals, and to be sworn in, Bobby and I, along with the other marine volunteers, had to walk the gauntlet of jeering young men.

The crowd shouted at us, "Hey, you fools, you're gonna get your butts shot off in Korea. Stupid idiots! Wanna be tough guys, eh?"

The more the others jeered, the prouder we were to be different, special to be Marines. After we were sworn in, the sergeant told us to that we would board the train to San Diego at two thirty.

On the train, it didn't take us long to hook up with recruits from other states. They were from Texas, Arkansas, Michigan, Kansas, Iowa, New York and New

Jersey. I thought they were a motley looking crew, and I suppose they thought we Texans, and other Southerners, were a strange looking group.

On the train we played cards and swapped stories, each of us trying to impress the others with how tough we were. But all of that came to a screeching halt when we came to San Diego. A Sergeant, with a bus and driver, met us at the train station. The sergeant was anything but nice. His cursed us and called us s___ heads. It shocked our tender civilian feelings.

When we went through the gate at the Marine Recruit Depot, the sergeant stood up glared at us and shouted, "Now, your butts belong to us, so you better give your hearts to God."

That first night, they made believers out of us. We were lined up against a wall and stripped down to our underwear. Each one of the three Drill Instructors came nose to nose with us, to intimidate and bully us. They told us that they were thinking of killing all of us, because we were just a bunch of worthless trash from the civilian world. According to them, there was no hope of any of us making it as Marines.

I thought the DIs were going to kill us, because one of them threw a bayonet at one of the recruits and barely missed him. The recruit was so frightened that he sank to the deck in a dead faint. *These crazy marines are really intending to kill us.*

Actually, the DIs were trying to snap us out of our cheap civilian ways. At any rate that's what they later told us they were trying to do. Their plan seemed to work, for we jumped every time a DI barked. If they told us to go somewhere, we ran as fast as possible.

They kept us up all night that first night and early in the morning marched us to the chow hall. They gave us ten minutes to eat and be back in formation. The last man to get back in formation would suffer at the hands of the Drill Instructor. He was as mean as a snake, and I was not planning on being the last one to get back in formation.

I gobbled down a bowl of food, eating like a hungry pig from a trough. Then I raced back to line up with the platoon. I wasn't the first, but I wasn't the last.

The first week we were prodded, threatened, driven and pushed to our limits. The weeks went by and one day we were proud marines marching in the graduation parade.

After boot camp, I went through combat training at Camp Pendleton. One of the high lights of that time was a forced march with a seventy-pound pack to the top of a mountain the Marines called Nellie's Tit. Swede Pederson and I were the first to reach the peak. We tied as we raced to be the first. Later on, Swede and I would play football together for the Jacksonville Navy Flyers.

After a tough week of combat training at Camp Pendleton, we were given liberty (a weekend pass). My friend, MacDonald, had a cousin who worked for Walt Disney in Hollywood. He invited Mac up for the weekend, and Mac invited me to go with him.

It was heady stuff being in Hollywood for a weekend. We had just spent the week sleeping in foxholes and eating C-rations.

Being in Hollywood was like a dream. MacDonald' cousin had two middle school daughters and an eight-year-old son. They had a swimming pool in the back yard and a spacious beautiful house. Bob Hope lived down the street from them and other movie stars were in the neighborhood.

Television was new, and they let us eat on TV trays while watching programs. They served us like we were celebrities, and we lapped it up. It was tough leaving this kind of life in Hollywood and getting back into the rough and disciplined life of combat training.

When we told our buddies back at Camp Pendleton that we had spent the weekend in Hollywood, they just looked at us in disbelief.

While I was at Camp Pendleton, a peace treaty, of a sort, was signed in Korea to bring the open war to a close. Therefore, many of us high school graduates were sent to technical training schools.

Playing Football for the Navy

After an eight day furlough, I went to the Jacksonville Naval Base for training as an ordnance technician.

While there, I met Jack Turner who was to become one of my friends. Jack played high school football and later played for the University of Arkansas. At Arkansas, he encountered some tough times and left the school to join the US Marines.

One day as we were standing in the chow line, Jack told me that Jacksonville Navy had a football team, and he was planning on going out for the team. He said, "Why don't you go with me. I'm sure they'll need some marines on the team."

"Sure, why not? Count me in. They may need a Turner-Turman one two punch."

I told Swede Pederson about the team, and he said he wanted to try out also. We reported for the football tryouts. All three of us made the team. Jack and Swede played at the guard position, and I was a running back.

During that time, football players usually played offense and defense. In one of our first games, we played a new college team at that time, Florida State. On defense, I played corner back. On one play, I noticed that the quarterback zeroed in on the wide receiver. Timing his throw, I bolted in front of the wide receiver and intercepted the pass and ran for a touchdown. The quarterback was Lee Corso. Each time I see him on TV, I think about that "Pick-six."

Playing football for Jacksonville Navy was a lot of fun. We were a mediocre team, but several times, we rose up to play beyond ourselves. Some of the teams we played had All-Americans on the line-up. One team, Ft. Belvoir, had seven All-Americans on their squad.

The Tennessee All-American and Heisman Trophy runner-up, Hank Lauricella, was one of the running backs on the Ft. Belvoir team. As a high school student, I remembered listening to the Cotton Bowl when Hank led the Vols to a win.

The night before the game, it was reported that Hank had spent the evening smoking cigars and drinking cocktails at the Officer's Club on the Jacksonville base.

A memorable time came in the game, when Ft. Belvoir marched the ball down to our two- yard line. Lauricella tried four times to smash through the line to score, but my friend, Jack Turner, stopped him cold.

After the third time, he got out of the pile, kicked the turf, apparently incensed that he couldn't get in to score and swaggered back to the huddle. The fans all rose to their feet in anticipation of a fourth down try. Most everyone knew that Hank was going to try again to get in and over Jack Turner.

Hank raced toward the same hole and took a flying leap trying to get over the pile. Jack, and that side of the line, smacked him down. Hank got up enraged that he couldn't score on a rag-tag Navy team. Even though we lost the game 19-0, we considered it a victory in many respects. We had taken the ball down within their ten-yard line three times, only to fumble it, or fail to get in to score.

In the first quarter, I raced down the middle for a pass. An elbow in the back of my head left me in a daze that lasted until half-time. I probably had a slight concussion. Wisely, the coaches would not let me back in the game.

A Weekend Pass

While playing football for the Jacksonville Navy Flyers, the team had a free weekend. My football buddy, Swede, and I decided to go to Gainesville and see the Gators play. Since we were hitch-hiking, we decided to wear our khaki Marine uniforms. We discovered that wearing our uniforms helped us get a ride when hitch-hiking.

By the time we arrived in Gainesville, it was pouring down a lot of liquid sunshine. Our khaki uniforms were soaked. We had to walk through the town to get to the stadium. Along the way, we passed several college dormitories. Something happened that caught us by surprise.

Students in the men's dormitories began to yell insults and make fun of us. Enraged, we challenged them to come out and fight us. This only intensified their mocking and insulting us. Disgusted, we walked on to the stadium.

The dormitory incident soured us so that it was hard to enjoy the game. Not only that, more rain came down to keep us soaked.

After the game, we walked back to the downtown area. As we were crossing the street, at a red light, a man in a new, black car stuck his head out the car window. He said, "Hey Marines, how about a ride?"

We were still sensitive and wary because of our past treatment. I said to Swede, "If he tries anything, let's slug 'im."

The man pulled his car over to the curb near where we were standing. He smiled broadly, as he got out of the car. "Hey Marines, it's good to see you. I have a son stationed in Europe at this time. I thought of him when I saw you. Have you eaten? If not, I know a place a couple of blocks down the street, a boarding house. They serve good food. Hop in and we'll go down and try it out, okay?"

I glanced at Swede and nodded, and he mouthed an affirmation. We were hungry and it sounded too good to turn down. We climbed into the man's car.

On the way to the boarding house, the man asked, "Where's your hometowns?"

After telling him where we were from, he said, "You know I spent some time in the army during the Second World War. I know how it feels to be in a town and not know anyone."

After arriving at the boarding house, we went into the dining room that had a long table that was full of guests. The guests, many of them students, were shoveling in the food. They paid no attention to our presence.

Our new friend found the lady in charge and gave her some money. He turned to us, "Listen, I've got to go somewhere. You all go ahead and eat. Here's my card. If you need anything get in touch me."

This Good Samaritan nodded toward us. "You all have a good weekend. Hope to see you sometimes. Take care."

We never saw our new friend again, but over the years he has not been forgotten. I still remember how this man's act of kindness melted the anger and resentment that I felt toward the college students and the town. Several times, I've had the opportunity to do acts of kindness toward strangers, like this man did to two Marines in a college town. He set the example for us.

Storming the Beaches of Florida and Puerto Rico

When Jack, Swede and I graduated from ordnance school, we had the top scores in our class. We could choose where we wanted to go from the options they gave us. Jack and I chose the Marine Air Station at Opa Locka, Florida. We had played Opa-Locka Marine Base in football, and we were impressed with the base and its location near Miami and its beaches.

In choosing Opa-Locka Marine Air Station, we made a good choice. It was a liberty loving station. Yes, it was a Marine Air Base, but a holiday like atmosphere pervaded the base. Marines were going out every night that they had liberty, if they had money.

After several months in Opa Locka, we went to Roosevelt Roads, Puerto Rico on maneuvers. We lived in tents outside the air base. One evening, one of my boot camp buddies, MacDonald, and myself, decided to go outside camp and check out the surroundings. My older and wiser friend, Jack Turner, warned me, "Hey, be careful and stay out of trouble. You can get in trouble real fast outside the camp here."

Mac and I put on our khaki uniforms and took off to see what we could find. The first place we came to was an enlisted men's club for the Navy personnel in the area. We swaggered into the club to see what the "Swabbies" were up to. Several sailors were sitting around drinking, and they gave us a cordial welcome and invited us to join them.

We joined them and they bought us a round of cocktails. Unaware of how much alcohol was in the drinks, we drank several with the friendly sailors. One of the sailors said, "You Marines are tough men. It's a honor to drink with you. Let me buy you another round of drinks."

After about seven or eight rounds we were drunk as skunks. I don't even remember leaving the club. Jack and some of our Marine buddies found us, later on, wandering around outside the camp ranting and raving like wild men. They took us to our tent and put us in our racks.

I awoke the next morning with my buddy, Jack, yelling at me, "Joey, you gotta get up or you're in trouble. The top sarge is coming round to check on our tents."

I crawled out of my rack, and I never felt so bad in my life. My head was hurting, and I felt like I wanted to throw up, but couldn't. My body hurt all over. I knew that I would be in big trouble if I didn't move out, so I stumbled to the shower tent and took a cold shower. That revived me.

I barely made it through the duties of the day. It was a terrible day, and I vowed that I would never take another drink. That experience made a believer out of me about being a teetotaler.

We came back to Opa-Locka in early July and resumed our schedule of work. One of the duties that our ordnance section was assigned too was spotting for the Marine fighter planes who did strafing and bomb runs in the swamp, located about twenty miles from Opa Locka. Sergeant Charles chose me to go with him three times. I really enjoyed getting off the base and getting out in the wilds of the swamp.

One day while we were in the swamp, Sergeant Charles said, "How'd you like to catch an alligator?"

"Catch an alligator? I don't think so."

"Don't worry, I'm not talking about a grown alligator."

"Here," he said, "See this pole and line. It's simple. Just tie this piece of meat to the end of the line and put it into the water see what happens."

I followed his instructions and within thirty seconds or less, I felt a strong tugging on the line, and I yanked it out of the water. On the end of the line was a baby alligator who had chomped down on the meat and would not let go. It was so much fun, that I ended up catching three more.

When I wasn't spotting for the planes, I played with the baby alligators. I had to be careful, because they would bite your hands with their sharp little teeth. It was so much fun playing with them that I took two of them back to the base to show my buddies.

After a day of playing with the alligators, they got away, and we could never find them. I can only imagine that those gators ended up twelve-foot monsters in somebody's back yard canal.

During early August, Jack and I began to think about football season. Opa Locka disbanded its football team, so we talked to the Special Services Officer about playing football for another Marine base. He suggested we play for the Cherry Point Marines, so we began the process to transfer to Cherry Point.

From the Hospital to the Football field

My buddies, Jack Turner, Gene Robinson and I transferred from the Marine Air Station in Opa Locka, Florida to Cherry Point, North Carolina to play football for the Cherry Point Marine Flyers. Jack played guard and Gene and I were running backs. Gene played college football for Lenoir Rhyne College where he, and his twin brother, were named Little All Americans.

In 1982, Gene, and his twin brother, Jerry, were inducted into the Lenoir Rhyne Sports Hall of Fame.

We felt like we were football's gift to Cherry Point, but after we arrived and reported for practice, we knew we had to earn our place on the team, like everyone else. The team's coach, Captain Chick Whalen, played for an Ivy League team and seemed to be partial to players east of the Mississippi.

I plunged into practice with a determination to nail down a starting position on the team. The first stringer who played ahead of me played for a small college in Pennsylvania. He was a sturdy-built hard driving running back who had already been selected for the starting role. I ran the hundred a step faster than he did.

In the first three games, I played only a few minutes in each game, but Jack got in a lot of playing time. I wasn't happy at all about the situation. I played first string at Jacksonville Navy and sitting on the bench was not something I had envisioned. Besides that, Coach Whalen seemed to be on my case.

One day in practice, he called me to come over to the kick-off return team. I jogged over. He called out to me, "When I call you, don't come with that little Texas-jog of yours."

I didn't like it, but I said nothing. After all, he was a captain and the coach of the team. On the Saturday that we played the Camp Lejeune Marines, I returned a kick-off down to their thirty-yard line. Two times I went into a swarm of would be tacklers, but juked them to emerge running for the goal. The kicker finally brought me down.

Coach Whalen liked that run, so he put me in to run the ball several more times. I made several first down runs. The next week in practice, he told me, "Turman, you're gonna play a lot in Saturday's game."

I practiced hard in anticipation of playing against one of the top service teams. They had several All-Americans on the starting line-up. Thursday during practice, I felt like the bottom dropped out of me. By the time practice was over, I was a sick puppy. Jack said, "Joey, you gotta go to the infirmary. You're as hot as a six-shooter."

He walked me over to the infirmary, and a nurse took my temperature. It was a hundred and three. She checked my throat and said, "Wow, Marine, you're gonna go right into the infirmary, now."

I said, "I gotta practice football tomorrow and get ready for Saturday's game."

"You're not going to be practicing or playing any football Saturday. Come on, we're checking you in and getting you a penicillin shot."

I looked at Jack and he just shook his head. He turned before he left, "Joey, follow doctor's orders and get yourself well."

They put me in bed and gave me several penicillin shots before they put me on the pill routine. Friday, after football practice, Jack came to visit me. He said, "We had a light work-out with no pads and ran through some plays. Coach Whalen, along with most of the staff, were not there. Joey, I don't think anyone missed you."

By Friday night I was feeling great. I asked Jack to bring over my khaki uniform and hang it on the end of my bed. I had something in mind. After the evening meal, I spoke to the head nurse. "I want to go to the game tomorrow and root for my team. Would you ask the doctor if I can attend the game?"

The nurse looked at me without an ounce of sympathy. "No, I'm not going to ask the doctor. You're gonna be here for three or four more days. Forget about going to any football game."

With each passing hour I felt better. By Saturday morning, I felt like I could take on the world. I really wanted to take on the Navy. Since the Navy provides the medical support and chaplains for the Marines, the infirmaries and chapels on Marine bases are operated by Navy personnel.

I knew that it would not be wise to have a head-on confrontation with the Navy personnel. I had another plan. At twelve noon, I noticed that there was a change of shift for the nurses. During the changing of personnel, there was usually five or ten minutes when no one was at the nurses' duty station.

I knew that the football team reported to the dressing room just after twelve, and the game started at two. With that in mind, I waited for the changing of nurses. At twelve, when the nurse left her station, I jumped up and put on my uniform, walked out of the infirmary and down to the football stadium, where I dressed out in my football uniform.

While I was out on the field catching punts during warm-up time, I noticed the game-doctor was my doctor at the infirmary; so I raced over to our bench and put on my helmet. I didn't want him to recognize me.

The game got underway, and I stood near our bench bouncing around. I felt great and wanted to get in the game. Midway in the first quarter, Craig, the running back ahead of me, was down on the field. Coach Whalen called out, "Turman, get in there."

In the huddle, the quarterback called my play. I hit the line with all the energy that was in me, found a seam and took the ball fifteen yards. The quarterback dialed my number again. I raced for another first down. When I came back to the huddle, I was winded and hoping that my number wouldn't be called. But it was, so I mustered all the strength that remained in me and hit the line for a pick -up of eight. Coach Whalen and our bench were all jumping up and down.

When I came back to the huddle this time, I had nothing left. Fortunately, the fullback got the call. During the play, I just stood still. Jack saw that I was out of it and motioned for the Coach to get me out of the game. At the next time-out, Jack told Coach Whalen that I had just come out of the hospital. The coach came over and put his hand on my shoulder. He could see that I was done for the day.

After the game, I trudged to the locker room and changed into my uniform. I felt horrible. Jack walked me back to the infirmary. The nurse confronted me, "Where've you been?"

"I went to the football game."

"You're gonna get court martialed for leaving the infirmary and disobeying orders."

I was so beat that I didn't care. "Okay, so what."

I took off my uniform and crawled back in bed.

The infirmary dismissed me the following Tuesday. The head nurse reminded me that I would be court martialed.

Tuesday afternoon I reported for football practice. The next morning we went to the base theater to see the game film. When the film came to my going into the game and hitting the line, Chick Whalen couldn't say enough about me, He replayed my hitting the line four or five times, saying, "Running backs, this is how you're to do it. Look, this is how you're to hit the line."

Coach Whalen was for me now, and it felt good to have the coach on my side. After practice one day, I told Coach Whalen, "Coach, the Navy wants to court martial me. Tomorrow I'm to go before the Colonel in view of a court martial."

"Turman, don't worry about it. The Colonel is a Marine. Tell him you came out of the infirmary to play football for the Marines."

The following morning, I shined my shoes, sharpened up my uniform and went before the Colonel. I stood at attention before his desk. He said, "Private Turman, is it true that you left the infirmary without permission to attend a football game?"

"Yes sir."

"Why did you do that?"

"I went to play football for the Marines, Sir."

"Get outta here."

"Yes sir!"

I left the Colonel's office free from any threat of a court martial. Score one for the Marines over the Navy!

Leaning into a Left Hook

When football season was over, we Marines who were assigned to special services, had nothing to do all day, except to sweep out the gym, and keep the athletic equipment in order. Life became boring. My friend Jack and I worked out in the gym every day to keep in shape.

One day I was punching a heavy boxing bag when two Marines came over to where I was working out on the bag.

"Hey, how about sparing with my buddy here," one of them said.

"Yeah, sure I'll be glad too."

After we got in the ring with our gloves laced on, I sensed that it was not going to be a friendly sparring match. My opponent wanted a live target to punch on and take out.

My hunch proved right, for when the word was given to start, the man came out swinging, trying to take me out. I had boxed as an amateur in Texas, so I knew enough to avoid some of his punches. He was a tall, long-armed Marine and his flailing punches backed me into a corner.

When he backed me into a corner, I fought back like a cornered tiger. I threw a wild uppercut and hit the guy square on the chin. He went down like a sack of potatoes. I was more surprised than he was. He stayed down for several minute, to get the cob webs out of his head. I went over, patted him on the shoulder and climbed out of the ring.

At that time, I wasn't aware that Captain Chick Whalen, my football coach and athletic director for the base, saw the sparring session. He rushed over to me and said, "Turman, you're gonna be the next middle weight champion of the Marines Corp."

Somehow or another, I was dumb enough to believe him. Several days later, Captain Whalen told me that he had arranged for me to box one of the top middle weights in the Marines, who was also stationed at Cherry Point. I had a week to get ready for the fight.

My friend Jack agreed to be in my corner. That week, he told me, "Joey, you're no boxer. I don't know why you're doing this, but I'll be in your corner."

"I think I can take this guy out. Don't worry."

Some of my friends on the football team came to me for assurance. "Turman, we're gonna bet on you. Can you beat this guy?"

"Sure, I can. I wouldn't be climbing into the ring with him, if I didn't think I could beat him."

I really thought I could beat this Marine middle weight contender who had had fifty-five fights and had won most of them. Someone shared this information with me after the fight. He later became the Marine Middleweight Champion.

Now I had fought some as an amateur in Texas, but I had never faced a fighter who could throw a left hook. Most amateurs don't know how to handle a left hook. They don't see it coming.

This middle weight contender had a terrific left hook, and in the first round he uncorked his left hook. One minute deep into the first round, I was down on the canvass wondering where the punch came from. I got up in plenty of time. I had too. My buddies were all yelling at me to get up and fight.

In the middle of the second round, bam, another left hook put me down on the canvass. Again I got up in time. I tried to land my right hand, but my opponent slipped away to counter punch. He put me down in the third round, but I made it through the fight without getting knocked out.

I was thoroughly beaten, but more than that, I felt humiliated. I had let down my buddies. I had assured them that I would win, and they had put their money on me. Now, some of them would be short for the rest of the month.

After the fight, I didn't want to meet my old football buddies. I put in a request to go overseas, so I signed up to go with the USS Coral Sea on NATO maneuvers in the European Theater. My buddy Jack had been discharged and went home to play for the Memphis State Tigers. I had no reason to stay at Cherry Point.

Getting Out of Dodge

I was assigned to go with Marine Air Group 122, on the Coral Sea as an aviation ordinance man. I didn't know anyone in my new outfit.

I heard the top sarge say to one of his staff, "Turmans a jock." He was really saying that they couldn't expect much out of me, for they considered "Jocks" to be spoiled, pampered Marines and not of much use.

In a sense they were right, for we jocks ate at the infirmary with the nurses, doctors and officers. We were treated special; however, I had been trained as an ordinance man and would carry my share of the weight.

We flew to Jacksonville Naval Air Station and took a bus to the Mayport Naval Base, where the USS Coral Sea was anchored. It was a beautiful monster. I never realized an aircraft carrier was so large.

We Marines boarded carrying our sea bags on our shoulders. We were assigned to our racks and shown our working compartment.

The first thing to happen to the "Jock" was that I was put on mess duty. As soon as I put down my sea bag, I was told to report to the mess hall. Mess duty is no fun. You get up before others, and you work long after your buddies are relaxing in their racks.

I determined to do a good job, and I made a good mess hall worker. Growing up on a farm, I had a good work ethic. One of the side benefits of working in the mess hall was that you could eat as much as you wanted. On the days when we had ice cream, we mess hall workers ate two or three ice cream sandwiches. Whatever we had special, we managed to set apart extra for ourselves to snack on.

When we dropped anchor in Barcelona, we all were anxious to get on shore and see the city. While we were in a port, we rotated duty, one day on and one day off. I had duty the first day in port. Going about my duties, I was told to report to the chaplain. Wondering what it was all about, I went to the chaplain's office.

The chaplain was brief. He said, "I'm sorry Marine, but we just got word that your brother who was a former Marine has been killed. I don't have any particulars. If I can be of any help, let me know."

I wandered out of the office in a daze. Which one of my brothers was killed? Three of them were former Marines. Was it Charlie, Gene or Pat? Charlie and Gene had served in WWII and Pat had served in Korea. Walking in a semi-daze, I ended up in our work compartment. My top sergeant had heard about the death. He said, "Turman, why don't you take the day off."

I went to our sleeping compartment and laid down on my rack, and I went over in my mind each one of my Marine brothers. Up until this time, there had not been a death in our immediate family. It was going to be tough on the family, and I would not be there.

About an hour later, the chaplain sent word for me to come to his office again. When I walked in, he glanced up and said, "Your brother Pat was the one killed in a car accident. Sorry about that."

Pat had served four years in the Marines. He had spent more than a year in Korea, during the worst part of the war. I remembered the last night on furlough, before I came back to Cherry Point. Pat was still single. Being between jobs, he stayed on the farm with Mama and Papa.

On my last night at home, I watched TV programs with Pat and my younger brothers. We made small conversation, in and around the programs. Pat hardly ever initiated conversation; he was a counter-puncher conversationalist. He took the conversation and masterfully turned it into something interesting or funny.

Pat spent his last year in Korea, during the bloodiest time of the war. He seldom mentioned anything about the war. One time, in a conversation about the different branches of service, he said, "When my outfit was overrun by the Chinese Communist, I escaped and attached myself to an Army outfit. For a time, I wore army clothes. I didn't like it, but I had no choice."

Other than that remark, we knew little or nothing about Pat's time in Korea.

While I was watching TV that last evening, my high school buddy, Bobby, came by and wanted me to go out with him to date his girlfriend' friend.

There was a lot of pressure put on me to go on this date, because the girl was already in his car sitting in the back seat. Bobby felt sure that I would go with him. He said, "Come on Joe, we'll be back after a few hours."

I knew that once we were out, we wouldn't be back until late in the evening. I declined, "No, I can't go. I'm going to spend this last evening with my family."

Bobby voiced his disappointment, "Joe, this girl really wants to date you. She set aside her evening to double-date. She'll be hurt."

I didn't give an inch, "No, I can't go. I'll see you on my next furlough."

As I thought of that last night, I was glad I stayed home with Pat and the family. Pat was a lot of fun to hang out with. He always had something unique and funny to say. His humor was dry and inconspicuous. He didn't say much, but when he spoke everyone listened. He had keen observations about life.

Now, Pat was gone. I would never see him again in this world. That last night that I spent at home with Pat and family was and always will be special.

Bar Room Brawl in Barcelona

The Coral Sea docked in Barcelona for six days. On the fifth day, I decided to go on liberty to get off the ship. I got off the liberty launch with a group of sailors and Marines and followed them downtown. I went into a restaurant and ordered steak, fries and a coke.

Across the street from the restaurant was a large dance hall. A large crowd of sailors and Marines crowded into the place. Since the manager of the restaurant spoke some English, I asked him, "What's going on over there?"

"It's a dance hall with a lot of girls. They have a good band. Why don't you go? You'll enjoy the band music."

I walked over to the dance hall and stood on the edge of the crowd. After a few Glenn Miller songs, the band struck up "Anchors Away." The sailors all stood, yelled and clapped. Then the band played the Marine Corp Hymn.

Even though we Marines were out- numbered, we yelled and clapped more enthusiastically, to make up for our lesser presence. In the middle of the hymn, two sailors got out on the dance floor and began to dance. This irreverent act was too much for me to take. Before I could put a handle on my emotions, I picked up a chair and knocked the two sailors off the dance floor.

Pandemonium broke loose. One Marine threw a chair, and another one threw his drink. Then Marines and sailors began to slug it out on the dance floor. The Shore Patrol showed up in about three minutes to save the dance hall from been ripped apart.

The commander on duty with the Shore Patrol shouted out “Who started this?”

A sailor pointed toward me and said, “He did. He threw a chair. Commander, let me take him on. I want a piece of him.”

I glared at him. “You can have a piece of me Swabbie.”

The commander said, “There’ll be no more of this.” He said to me, “You come on. I’m taking you down to the Shore Patrol Station.”

At the station, the commander said, “Why did you do that?”

“Those sailors were dancing to the Marine Corp hymn, sir, and that insulted me.”

The commander was a man in his late thirties with a kind-looking face. He looked at me for several seconds. “Didn’t you receive word a few days ago that your brother was killed in an accident?”

“Yes sir. He was a Marine and served in Korea.”

“I see. You know I’m not going to charge you with anything. I tell you what. You get on that liberty launch and go back to the ship. Stay out of trouble, okay?”

While in other ports, I enjoyed times more interesting, and not so action-packed.

Hanging Out with the Turks

When the Coral Sea came to port at Istanbul, the ship's radio played the tune "Istanbul, Constantinople" over and over. Mike, a six-foot-three Marine from Detroit, and I, decided that we would take our time of liberty away from the downtown area, where all the bars and night clubs were located.

We wanted to see the real face of Istanbul, so we started walking away from downtown. Not having any idea where we were going, we came to a middle-class-looking neighborhood. We heard the sound of oriental music coming from behind a high-walled yard. Curious, we tried to look over the gate to see what was going on. Evidently, the host saw us trying to see over the fence, so he opened the gate and invited us to come in.

The large yard was crowded with people, and a platform was standing in the middle of the crowd with dignitaries sitting on it. The host motioned for us to sit on the platform also. We hesitated, for we saw that some of the dignitaries were high-ranking Turkish officers. The host said to us, "You American Marines. We friends with you in Korea. You come."

We tentatively took our seats on the platform with the officers, who had enough brass on their uniforms to be admirals or generals. As soon as we were seated, servants came bringing us plates of food and drinks.

The host spoke a few words of English, but besides him, no one else could speak a word that we could understand. The officers on the platform tried to communicate with us, but soon gave up. We mutually could not understand one another.

The host introduced us, or at least we thought he did. He motioned for us to stand up, and the crowd gave us a round of applause. Even though we were given seats of honor, sitting with distinguished looking men, we felt uncomfortable. If you can't understand the language, you feel isolated and cut off from others around you. I looked at Mike and I could tell that he felt like I did…out of place. He whispered to me, "Let's get outta here."

"Yeah, okay, but we've got to stay long enough so that we don't insult this man. He was nice enough to invite us to come in."

After about an hour, I whispered to Mike, "When the band finishes this piece, let's go. But first, we've got to get permission from the host."

When the band finished its string music presentation, we stood up and walked over to the host. We bowed, shook his hand, and said, "We must go to our ship."

The host understood and shook our hands in a warm manner. He motioned to the people, and they stood and applauded, as we made our way to the gate. *Where else in the world could two Marine privates be treated like heroes with admirals and generals looking on.*

Homeward Bound

The USS Coral Sea pointed its bow toward the USA and Norfolk. I could feel the excitement sweeping over the ship. Sailors and Marines talked to one another more than usual. There was a festive spirit aboard ship. The ship radio played cheerful and lively music.

The last night aboard the USS Coral Sea, I had deck watch. I had a certain route that I was to cover on my watch. At the place where I turned around to retrace my walking route, I met another Marine on watch. When we met we spent five minutes or so talking.

That last night the moon was full, and a gentle breeze blew across the deck. It was a beautiful night to be out on the deck of a carrier cruising toward home port. Fifteen minutes before my watch was over, I spent more time than usual talking with my fellow Marine guard.

Suddenly, my Marine friend said, “Attention!” I turned to look behind me. The ship’s Captain, Captain David MacDonald, was standing within four feet of me. I didn’t hear or see him approaching us. He said, “It’s a nice night, isn’t it men?”

“Yes sir, it sure is.”

Captain MacDonald proceeded to carry on conversation with us, asking us where we came from and what did we think about the six months cruise. After finishing the conversation, he said, “Men, be careful. You’re not supposed to get together and talk while you’re on guard duty, okay?”

“Yes sir, Captain. Thank you, sir.”

Through the many years, I've never forgotten Captain MacDonald. He later became the Chairman of the Joint Chiefs of Staff.

The USS Coral Sea arrived at its home port, Norfolk, in early September. We Marines gathered together our baggage and continued on to Cherry Point.

I was already thinking about my coming discharge from the USMC in the coming January.

Days of Transition

After four months at Cherry Point, I was discharged honorably from the Marines on January 15, 1956, three years after I was sworn in. I realized that I probably would never see my Cherry Point Marine buddies again. I told them, "So long, maybe I'll see you somewhere, sometimes or someplace."

Catching a Greyhound bus, I made the long journey back to Tyler, Texas. From the Tyler Bus Station, I hitch-hiked to Noonday, which is eight miles south of Tyler. My ride let me off on State Highway 155, at the crossroads going to the Turman farm. I walked the mile to our house with my sea bag on my shoulder.

When I came up to the lane leading down to our farm house, I saw Papa, and my younger brothers, trying to push his truck out of a muddy ditch. When I approached them, they all looked up, embarrassed at my coming in and finding them in such an awkward situation. "Hey, Josefus. Welcome back! Go on up and see Mama and we'll be up in a minute."

It seemed like I had never being away. Papa getting his truck in the ditch and having to be pushed out was happening when I left three years ago.

Mama gave me a big hug and displayed more enthusiasm on seeing me than all the others put together. That was no surprise to me, for the men in our family did not show their emotions.

After a week of enjoying Mama's cooking and hanging out, I got a job working as a carpenter's helper. Working five days a week, on a regular eight to five shift, I had time to start working out to get back in shape for football. My plans were to play football for some university. Baylor was foremost in my mind, because I thought that I would have the best chance of playing.

I drove down to Waco one day to check out the campus. While there, I talked to the Athletic Director. He encouraged me to come on down and come out as a walk-on. He asked two football players to show me around the campus. Del Shofner was one of the players.

I enrolled for the Spring Quarter, and my tuition was paid for by the GI Bill. That quarter was an enjoyable experience for me. The relaxed schedule gave me time to get acquainted with the campus and make a few friends. It was a pleasant experience.

That spring I worked out with the track team, and that experience gave me time to get in better shape and to increase my speed.

For the coming summer, I was recruited to sell Bibles for The Southwestern Company in Michigan. My brother Chet went with me. We were assigned to sell in Adrian, Michigan for the summer months. It was an exciting time. Neither one of us had a car, so a lot of our time was spent in walking to the different neighborhoods.

Chet sold a family Bible to a young couple who really liked him and invited him to come back and visit them. He went back often to their house and helped the family with some of their house repairs.

We found a Southern Baptist Church and began to attend on Sundays. Most of the people in the congregation were Southerners. Since a number of young people sang in the choir, they urged us to join the choir. Neither one of us could carry a tune, but we became choir members. Chet and I had a lot of fun kidding one another about our lack of musical talent.

One night, in the middle of June, we came back to our rented room around nine o'clock. The landlady told us that we were to call our home. We got our brother Dan on the phone, and he told us the sad news that our Grandma had passed away.

The news of Grandma's death saddened us, because Grandma had lived with us for years, and we loved her. Now, she was gone. Chet and I didn't say much to one another. We were afraid that we would lose it emotionally, if we talked about grandma; so, we went to bed with our individual sorrow.

After some time in bed, I could hear Chet crying. He was very close to Grandma.

The summer went by quickly, and we collected from those who had bought Bibles. It had been an interesting summer, but we barely broke even.

Quitting and Running

I returned to Baylor the first week in September and enrolled in my classes. Then I reported for football practice. At that time, freshman did not play on varsity teams, but they competed with other freshmen in the Southwest Conference.

I was not in great shape, but I was in good enough shape to make it through the first practices. When we ran fifty yard dashes, I usually came in first or second in each of these dashes. The coaches selected me to run the fullback position. I was surprised, but I think it was because I could block. In practice, I laid into the defenders trying to get to the quarterback.

One day in practice, I took a hard blow on my right thigh. Even though I had on thigh pads, the blow delivered by a helmet bruised my thigh. After practice, I talked to the trainer and he put me in a hot swirl pool and told me to take it easy for a few days. The next afternoon we had a full scrimmage. The coach sent me in to carry the ball. I told him that I had a bruised thigh and the trainer told me to lay off a few days. He looked angry and shouted, "Get the H_____ in there!"

The coach's anger and indifferent attitude toward my condition angered me. I raced in and ran the ball with all my might. It further aggravated my bruised thigh.

That coming Friday was a holiday, and the next football practice was slated for the following Monday. Three boys in my dorm were going to San Antonio for a long weekend. They invited me to go with them. Since my sister Bette lived in San Antonio, I decided to go with them to visit her.

Over the weekend, I smoldered with resentment about the coach's attitude toward me on the field. On the way back to Waco, I decided to quit the team. I would not go back to the locker room to turn in my equipment, and I would not talk to the coach. I would just quit. I resented being treated like a thing, and not a person.

That was a wrong decision. Over the years I've played back the scenario dozens of times. I really wanted to play college football, and I should have stuck it out. I could have made the team.

After I quit the football team, I was never happy at Baylor. I felt I had failed there, and I wanted to leave the campus. I drifted in my studies, and I couldn't wait until the Christmas holidays.

I spent Christmas with Mama, Papa and family in Noonday. It wasn't a good time for me, because I was still dissatisfied with how things had worked out at Baylor. In my mind, I went over the options in regards to my future. Each time I thought about continuing at Baylor, I negated it in my thinking.

When the holidays were over, I returned to Baylor like I was going to continue on as a student. After a few weeks on the campus, I packed up and left. My old Chevy had given up the ghost, so I had to hitch-hike wherever I was going. I decided on Houston.

Trying to Find A Way

Arriving in Houston, I found a cheap room in a boarding house and went to the unemployment office. They alerted me to construction jobs open with Brown & Root Construction Company. I went down to their home office and they immediately hired me. The company had a project repairing a bridge across the Brazos River in Central Texas.

While in the office, I met Jimmy from New York City. He had just recently been discharged from the Navy. Jimmy and I hit it off from the beginning. He was an adventuresome, fun-loving Irishman, and I was running from a failed college career. We were both seeking new adventures, and we were the same age.

The company told us where the construction project was located and told us to report to the foreman the day after tomorrow. Jimmy drove a beat up Ford, and he invited me to go with him to our new job. The job site was located a hundred and fifty miles northwest of Houston.

The men in the home office told us that we could rent a room in a small town eight miles from the construction site. Upon our arrival we found that it was a boarding house that fed breakfast and supper. We got a room with two single beds and lolled around in our room until the supper bell rang. We were two hungry young men, and we ate like it was going out of style.

The men on the job were friendly and helpful in getting us adjusted to our new jobs. They good-naturedly kidded Jimmy about being a Yankee from New York. "Hey Yank, are you a drug-store cowboy? How are you finding Texas? It's not like Broadway. Have you ever ridden a horse?"

Jimmy took their kidding with good humor. They sort of liked him, or they would not have joked around with him.

One day I was working on a barge doing some work on the side of the bridge. Heavy materials were put on the end of the barge that caused it to rise up standing on one end in the water. I was thrown off the barge into the water. The barge teetered in an upright position for a second, towering above me. Watching it, I wondered if it was going to fall on me or go the other way. In those few seconds, life seemed to be suspended in time, as I waited to see if the barge was going to fall my way and crush me in the water.

The barge settled slowly and somewhat gracefully away from me. Jimmy said, "Man, I was worried about you for a few seconds. That thing could've fallen on you."

After some time on the job, Jimmy said, "Hey Joey, how about us going to New York? We can make twice what we make here. My old man lives out in Queens and has a big house by himself. He and my Mom are divorced. We can stay with him and not have to pay any rent."

"Sounds good to me. When do we leave?"

Jimmy squinted as he looked up from his working posture, "Today's Thursday, so why don't we tell the foreman that we'll work until a week from tomorrow. That'll give them time to cut us our checks."

"Okay, I'll tell the foreman after work today."

Eight days later we threw our few clothes in the Ford and took off for New Mexico. Before we went to

New York, Jimmy wanted to visit his sister, Mary, who was stationed at Walker AFB in Albuquerque.

Even though Jimmy's old Ford didn't look like much of a car, it got us where we were going. The Ford didn't miss a beat on our way to Albuquerque, and we enjoyed seeing the wide open spaces.

Upon our arrival at the base, we made contact with Mary and set up a time to have dinner with her at seven. It was a pleasant time eating with Jimmy and Mary. I expected them to spend a lot of time talking among themselves about family matters, but they didn't. They did spend a few minutes speaking in low tones with one another, but most of the time I was included in the conversation.

Mary was a college grad and a lieutenant. She had been in the Air Force for two years. She spoke in proper English and appeared to be a highly disciplined person. Jimmy, on the other hand, was undisciplined in his personal habits.

During the progression of the evening, I picked up on the fact that Jimmy was the younger brother and Mary, as the older sister, felt she had to address some of his habits. Jimmy deflected her comments and, in a round-about-way, let her know that she was wasting her time trying to change him.

Mary found us a place to sleep at the base guesthouse. The next morning, we ate a leisure breakfast and headed toward New York.

On our way driving toward the east, we passed near Waco in the late afternoon. I said to Jimmy, "I've got an uncle and aunt who live near here. Why don't we spend the night with them? Aunt Kate can really turn out some good food."

Jimmy replied, “Okay, I’m ready for some home cooking. Let’s do it.”

Uncle Pop

Uncle Pop and Aunt Kate lived on a farm and ranch about five miles outside of a small town called West. Uncle Pop was a tall, heavy built Texan who wore cowboy boots and a white Stetson hat. He was a horse and cow trader and was well-known around that area.

Aunt Kate was a quiet, hard-working lady who had raised two children and had kept the home fires burning. She tended to a chicken house full of chickens and gathered dozens of eggs each day. She carefully nurtured twenty or more half-grown fryer chickens. Fried chicken was her specialty, along with creamed potatoes, brown gravy and biscuits.

On the way out to Uncle Pop's place, I tried to prepare Jimmy for meeting Uncle Pop. "Jimmy, now Uncle Pop is a Texan who's spent his life around horses and cows. He'll tell some tall tales, and he's good at it. But he's got a big heart, and he'll take us in and treat us with the best that he has."

We arrived about an hour before supper time. After greeting us, Aunt Kate began to prepare some fried chicken for supper. While Aunt Kate cooked up a delicious meal, Uncle Pop entertained us with some of his tales.

Jimmy didn't know anything about farm and ranch life, since he was raised in New York City. Uncle Pop, sensing that he had a city slicker in his audience, cranked out some of his favorite stories:

"Now, Kate, as you noticed, has a chicken house full of chickens. She sells eggs every day, except Sunday. Pete Ford comes by to pick them up. One day I told Kate,

'I'm going to get those hens laying more eggs, I mean laying more than any other hens lay.'"

Kate asked me, "How you gonna do that Pop?"

I said, "Give me some time to work on their nests and I'll show you."

"Well, I went into that chicken house and took each one of the hens' nests and I made a round hole in the bottom middle of the nest and attached a sack below the nest under the hole. The next day those hens would lay an egg and stand up and cackle-cackle and look down to see their egg that they had just laid. There was no egg there, since it had fallen into the sack beneath the nest. Those doggone hens would sit back down and lay another egg."

Jimmy eyes widened, "That was a great idea, Mr. Pop. How many eggs did they lay in a day?"

"Sometimes five or six," he said, with a straight face.

It was hard for me to keep from laughing out loud. I was about to burst trying to contain myself when Aunt Kate called us to eat supper.

Aunt Kate's supper was everything I said it would be…and more. Her chocolate pie put the finishing touches on the meal.

After the delicious supper, we went back into the living room to listen to more of Uncle Pop's tales. The good meal had invigorated him to launch out again on his repertoire of tales. To Uncle Pop's everlasting credit, we never got bored listening to him. Jimmy hung on every word and looked at Uncle Pop with a look of awe. It was like he was in the presence of a Buffalo Bill Cody, or some other western legend.

At eight o'clock, Uncle Pop closed out on his stories and said, "Boys, I've got to hear the news, and then we'll go to bed."

Jimmy looked at me with a look that said, *am I hearing him right? Go to bed* at *eight o'clock?*

When the news was over, Uncle Pop bid us good night. He said, "Kate will get you boys bedded down for the night. I'll see you in the morning."

Aunt Kate took us in and showed us our bed. She said, "If you need anything, let me know."

After Aunt Kate closed the door, Jimmy sat down on the edge of the bed. He slowly shook his head. "I ain't believing this," he said, "I've never been to bed at eight o'clock in my life."

"Jimmy, you ain't gonna believe it when Uncle Pop gets us out of bed at four o'clock."

"Are you kidding me?"

"No, trust me. He'll bang on that door at four o'clock."

Sure enough, exactly at four o'clock, Uncle Pop banged on our door. "Come on boys, up and at 'em. Breakfast in a little while."

I staggered to the bathroom and washed my face and brushed my teeth. Jimmy had not moved. He covered his head with a quilt and showed no signs of life. After putting on my clothes, I went over and shook him. "Jimmy, you gotta get up. Hear? You gotta get up."

Jimmy didn't move a muscle. I thought I heard a faint groan coming from the cover. I thought I would try to talk him up. "Jimmy, come on and get up. Aunt Kate is cooking eggs, bacon, sausage, gravy and biscuits with plenty of butter and jam."

Still no response from Jimmy. I thought I would try another strategy. "Jimmy, Uncle Pop is a high-tempered man. He's been known to come in and beat boys out of bed. He takes it personally when people don't get up. He thinks they're ignoring him, and it makes him mad. I'm telling you from experience; you better get up."

My strategy worked, for Jimmy poked his head out from the cover. "Are you serious?"

"Sure I'm serious. You better get moving. Time is running out on you."

Jimmy jumped out of bed, put on his clothes and washed his face. I never saw Jimmy brush his teeth. I guess the Navy was lax about that.

Breakfast was all that I said it would be. Jimmy ate like he never had a square meal. The more he ate, the more he smiled. After gulping down three cups of coffee, Jimmy was back in his usual good-natured form.

Before seven o'clock we were ready to get on the road. We said our thank you and good-byes to Uncle Pop and Aunt Kate and got on the road heading for New York.

New York, New York

The farther we drove north, the colder the weather. I felt cold all over, because the old Ford did not have a working heater. Jimmy stopped and bought him a bottle of wine to nip on to keep him warm.

Driving through the mountains of West Virginia, we stopped at a café to get coffee and a hamburger. The local men hanging around the café were a mean looking bunch. They gave us some hard looks. I told Jimmy, “Let’s get outta here while we can.”

We finished our hamburger, while we drove out of that small town that had snow covering its streets and roof tops. It was a dreary downtrodden looking town. I said to Jimmy, “I guess if I lived here, I’d be a mean-looking dude also.”

When we arrived in New York, there was a slight snow covering the roofs and trees. Jimmy’s father lived in a two-story house in Queens. He was an executive for a large publishing company. He did not give me a hearty welcome, for he was a quiet man. He just said, “Glad to meet you.”

I could sense that he and Jimmy had some differences that had never been settled. There was a tension in the air, when they were together. Jimmy and I each had a bedroom, and we spent the first few days catching up on our rest and trying to figure out our next move to find a job.

Jimmy knew a union boss in the construction business, so he got us a construction job. My job was an assistant to a brick layer. The brick layer worked me very hard. After a day’s work, I slept like a baby.

My job paid well, but often the weather was bad, and we didn't work. After a week without any work, I went job hunting in Manhattan. The first day of job-hunting, I found a job on Broadway with Mike Todd's United Artist Studio working in the mailroom. My job was to deliver letters in the Manhattan area.

In the interview, I was asked, "Do you know downtown New York?"

I said, "Sure."

They hired me, and I found my way around downtown by asking people on the streets and in the stores, where a certain store or office was located. Once I asked a man on the street, "Where's Macys?"

He looked at me to see if I was kidding. He said, "You don't know where Macys is? Just cross the street and look to ya right, okay?"

I worked at United Artists for six weeks and decided to look for work that paid more. Before I quit my job, I found a job working as a bartender at Schraff's Bar and Restaurant at Fifth Avenue and Thirteenth Street. My work was to prepare the cocktails and mixed drinks on the third floor. The waitresses came by and picked them up and served them in the cocktail lounge.

Many famous people from the United Nations, New York, and other places, patronized the cocktail lounge. A regular weekly customer was Bishop Sheen. I often watched him on TV. He was an excellent speaker and would hold you with his penetrating gaze and well-presented message. He always ordered an extra dry martini.

A bartender, who came from Boston, worked with me in preparing the drinks. He was an alcoholic. I say that because, when he came to work, he needed a drink to jump-start himself to do his work. He would whisper to me when he passed by, "Joe, get me a drink and put it in the usual place."

I fixed him his usual drink and put it in the same place at the corner end of the bar. He would sweep by, pick it up in one motion and drink it. It was against the rules for us to drink on the job, but I knew my friend would never make it without a drink.

After a month of living at Jimmy's dad's house, I decided to move out to a rented room. There was some tension in the air between Jimmy, and his dad, and I didn't want to be caught up in it.

I found a room, not far from Jimmy's house, in Queens. It was a two-story house that had an outside staircase leading to the rooms on the second floor. The only other renter was a quiet middle-aged man who came and went saying "hello" when he happened to meet me.

The landlady who was a grandmotherly-looking Jewish lady told me, "You're not to drink alcoholic beverages here."

The room fit my needs, and I went out and came in without seeing anyone. The only time I met the landlady was when I paid my rent.

One warm evening in early March, I discovered that I could go outside my window and with a little climbing get on the roof of the house. To get out of my room for a change, I would often sit perched on the roof looking out over the neighborhood. Sometimes people passing by on the sidewalk would glance up and see me staring down at them. They would walk on down the sidewalk looking back with a startled look on their faces.

During that time, I made contact with my friend, Sol, who lived in Brooklyn. He and I had served together in the Marines. He had just received his discharge after a four-year hitch.

Sol invited me to come have dinner with his family one Saturday afternoon. They lived in a flat, in a crowded neighborhood in Brooklyn. Sol's parents were in their late fifties, or early sixties. Sol was the oldest of four children.

The family treated me with respect, and they were very gracious in all their efforts to make me feel at home. The food was good, and I had a warm feeling toward the Jewish mother who had gone out of her way to prepare a meal for a Texas Gentile.

After we had eaten and visited with Sol's family for a while, Sol said, "Let's go dancing and spice up our evening."

"Okay, you lead the way. Sounds good to me."

We headed downtown to go to the Irish-American Dance Hall, which had a band and lots of single girls. On the way, walking down Broadway, we met Milton Hartsell, an old friend of mine from high school days. Milton was in his Air force uniform with another airman.

Milton couldn't believe it was a Tyler High School friend in the middle of Broadway. "Turman, what are you doing here?"

"Hartsell, I could ask you the same question. It looks like you're doing good."

"Ya, a little party time, you know, to keep up the morale."

Milton Hartsell went back to East Texas and Louisiana and became a sport's writer for several newspapers. He later wrote a book. He was dramatically converted in his later years in life and became a dynamic witness for Jesus.

Sol and I went on to the Irish-American and danced until late in the evening. After a sandwich at a café near Broadway, we went our separate ways.

A Life Changing Encounter

I was off work on Sundays. My free weekend started at three o'clock on Saturday afternoon, when I got off work. On Saturday evenings, I usually got together with Saul to see a movie, or to go dancing.

On this particular weekend, the last week in May, Sol was out of town and I had no one to go with me. Saturday evening I ate dinner at an Italian restaurant and later took in a movie. It was no fun doing things by myself.

On Sunday morning, I slept in until around eleven. I took a subway to downtown Manhattan and ate a large breakfast. While walking around, I noticed that a James Dean movie was playing on the corner of Forty-Second and Broadway. I walked around Times Square until the movie started at one o'clock.

When I got out of the movie around four o'clock, I didn't want to go back to my room; so I continued walking around Times Square. A street preacher was preaching on the corner of Forty-Second and Broadway. A crowd of people gathered around him and some of them were not so friendly. Several young men were throwing spit balls at him. The preacher ignored them.

After an hour or so walking around and enjoying the spring evening, I passed by Madison Square Garden. Hundreds of people were going in the Garden; many of them carrying Bibles. Glancing up at the marquee, I saw that the big attraction for the evening was the Billy Graham Crusade.

I knew that Billy Graham was in town, because the newspapers were filled with news about the coming crusade. The editorials speculated on the likely failure of Billy Graham's big-tent type revival meeting in sophisticated Gotham. The pundits on radio and TV were having a field day with the crusade. The cabbies were also talking about the meeting.

I stood for a moment debating on whether I would actually go in, or not. I glanced up at the marquee again. The word "free" caught my eye. Pay day was the coming Tuesday, and I was short on money. I could spend a free evening listening to a world famous preacher. Why not? I followed the crowd into the garden.

An usher told me that seats were available on the top balcony. I made my way up to the balcony and found a seat on the last row. The people around me were friendly and smiling. I relaxed and enjoyed listening to the singing of hymns that I had sung in church while growing up in Noonday, Texas.

George Beverly Shea, and the choir, led by Cliff Barrows, sang "How Great Thou Art." I enjoyed the music. Billy Graham came to the podium and began to speak. I listened closely to this preacher, because I had heard so much about him in the last few weeks.

As he spoke, I sensed that he was sincere, and his words had a ring of authority. He looked out at the crowd with a penetrating look, as if he was looking into your very soul.

About half way through his sermon, I began to feel uncomfortable. I had come to spend a free evening, and I had not thought about being confronted by the Spirit of God. And that was happening to me, as the Holy Spirit began to convict me of sin, righteousness and judgment to come. I wanted to leave, but I couldn't. It was like my shoes were nailed to the floor.

Billy Graham said something that grabbed my attention: "Tonight you can start over again in life. Jesus died for every sin you have ever committed, or ever will commit in the future. He will bury your sins in the uttermost depths of the sea and put them away as far as the east is from the west."

When the choir began to sing "Just As I Am," I bowed my head and in the best way I knew how to pray, I prayed: "Lord, I've messed up in life. I want to start over again. Please forgive my sins and come into my heart and be my Lord and Savior. I want to turn my life over to You."

In that moment something wonderful happened in my life. A terrible weight was lifted from my soul, and I felt clean and free. A warm joy spread over me. I didn't know all that was involved in this experience, but I knew that it was real and I wanted more of it.

I could hear the evangelist inviting those who wanted to profess Jesus as Lord and Savior to come forward. I left my seat to join dozens of others who were making their way down to stand in front of the podium.

I joined several hundred people standing in front of Billy Graham. He spoke to us for a few minutes, and then we were led backstage for counseling. A young man counseled me, but I don't remember a word that he said. He didn't connect with me, but he did give me a Gospel of John and a few tracts.

When I left Madison Square Garden, I made my way down to the corner of Forty-Second Street and Broadway to catch a subway to Queens. When I approached the corner, the street preacher was finishing up his message. He kept repeating, "Who'll step out for Jesus. Come stand by my side."

The voice of the Lord was clear as a bell to me: "Step out!"

I stepped out and stood by the side of the preacher for half a minute, or so, then I went to catch the subway to Queens.

Back in my room, I read a few verses from the Gospel of John and said a short prayer before I went to sleep. I knew that something wonderful had happened to me, and I would never be the same person.

Regrouping in Florida

Monday at noon, on my job, I told the manager that I would be leaving my job on Friday. He said, “You know, you’re a good worker. If you’ll stay, I would like to train you to be a manager.”

I said, “No, thank you. I’m going to Florida.”

He asked me to stay on for a few more days, so he could find someone to take my place. He was a nice person, and I agreed to stay longer.

Eight days after my commitment to follow Jesus, I boarded a Greyhound Bus for St. Petersburg, Florida. During my time in the Marines, I had gone to St. Pete a number of times to visit Jan, a girl that I met at Ocala, Florida. Her family had moved to St. Pete after she graduated from high school.

Jan was a nice girl and our dating was casual. Often we would go swimming at Silver Springs. In the evenings, we usually ended up at her house eating cookies and watching TV. So, when I wanted to get away from New York, I thought of St. Pete. It was a quiet and slow moving city, and I knew someone who lived there.

When I arrived in St. Pete, I bought a newspaper and looked for rooms for rent. A room near Spa Beach attracted my attention. It wasn’t far from downtown, so I walked to the address carrying my suitcase.

The landlady was a widow, who had spent most of her married life in Nashville, Tennessee. She engaged me in conversation to find out about me and my lifestyle. She seemed to be satisfied with me, so she showed me an upstairs room.

After I had unpacked, I laid down across the bed and went sound asleep. Waking up in the middle of the night, I pulled off my clothes and crawled back in bed. Around six in the morning, I heard the paper boy throwing papers on the street. When the paper plopped on the front porch of the two-story house, I heard Mrs. Maxwell go out and get it.

After eating breakfast in a fast food diner, two blocks from my rent house, I bought a paper and looked in the job section. A roofing company needed workers, as soon as possible, and they were paying decent wages. I returned to my room, changed into my work clothes and went to the address given in the paper. They hired me on the spot and wanted me to go on to the job in progress.

Two hours after been hired, I was on top of a house putting down shingles. The blazing sun soon made me sweat my shirt wet. Not realizing that I needed to keep on a wet shirt to avoid too much sun, I pulled off my shirt and worked bareback. After two hours in the hot sun, I began to black out. The men working with me helped me off the roof and poured some ice water on my head.

After I recovered, I worked on the ground for the rest of the day. After ten days with the roofing company, they laid me off because of lack of houses to roof.

Two days later, I went to work for a construction company building a power plant on Weedon Island, which was about ten miles from St. Pete. Hired as a carpenter's helper. I did everything the carpenters did, but received only half as much as they did, because I was not a member of the union.

One of the carpenters that was friendly and helpful to me was a man everyone called "Frenchy." I always enjoyed working with Frenchy, because he was good-natured and entertained me with a lot of interesting stories.

One rainy day while working on a platform, Frenchy fell thirty feet. I heard the dreadful plop sound of his body hitting the cement floor down below. They took Frenchy away in a company van, and I never knew whether he made it, or not. No one wanted to talk about it. When I asked someone how Frenchy was doing, they would say, "Oh, he'll make it okay."

Two weeks after my arrival in St. Pete, I called Jan and told her that I was in town. She said, "I'll come by and get you, and we'll go get a coke or something."

After she picked me up, she drove to the pier, and we walked out on it to a small café. We ordered a cold drink and talked for over an hour. She asked, "Why did you come back to St. Pete?"

"You're the only person I know in Florida, and I like the slow-paced life here in St. Pete. I want to date you again, of course."

A slight smile highlighted the dimples in her cheeks. "You don't know whether I'm available or not. You haven't corresponded with me in more than a year."

"I thought I would give it a try anyway. Well, are you available?"

"I'm dating an air force guy stationed in Georgia, but we're just dating."

"Do you like him?"

"Yeah, he's okay. Tell me what has happened in your life since you left Florida."

I told Jan about my conversion experience in New York City. I said, "I'm a new person now. Christ is my Lord and Savior, and I want my life to count for Him. Last Sunday I visited the Fifth Avenue Baptist Church, and I really liked it. Would you go with me this Sunday?"

Jan said, "I've visited that church before, but I really like a smaller church."

I began to attend the Fifth Avenue Baptist every Sunday. Whether Jan went to her smaller church, or not, I wasn't sure. Relating my conversion experience and my commitment to follow Christ seem to affect her. From that time, she seemed distant and cool in her feelings toward me. After that, I only saw her occasionally. She soon told me that she was dating her air force friend on a regular basis, so I never saw her again.

Fifth Avenue Baptist Church was a Bible-centered church, and I began to grow under the ministry of the Word coming from the pulpit and the Sunday School teachings. The Training Union group encouraged and challenged me to stand before others to make a presentation.

When I was given my first part to share in Training Union, I prayed, practiced and sweated in preparation to make the three minute presentation. Giving a talk before others somehow caused my heart to race, my throat to constrict and my knees to shake. It was awful. *There's no reason to be afraid. You can do it. They're all pulling for you.*

But all the self-counsel did not assuage the fear that I felt in standing before the class. I made myself do it. Even though my knees were indeed shaking, I somehow got through the presentation. After I finished, I felt elated because I had made it through my first presentation. It was a victory, a big victory for me. I could do it. The next time I stood before the class, I was stronger in speaking out.

The church had a good number of young people who participated in the church's programs. Some of the young people were dynamic Christian leaders who planned wholesome activities for our classes. It was through participating in these fun times, on the beach and other fellowships, that I realized young people can have a great time together without drinking, drugs and what else goes with it.

Calling, Commitment and College

On Sundays I attended church, came back to my room and made a bowl of soup with a sandwich. After that I usually did some reading or took a walk on the beach.

One Sunday in early August, I took a walk on the beach. A shark had attacked a girl, while she swam out from the beach some months before, so there were no swimmers or sun-bathers. A few fishermen cast out their lines at the far end of the beach.

Having the beach practically to myself, I walked along thinking of what I had heard from the sermon and Sunday School lesson. The teachings of the Bible excited me. As I thought about spiritual truths, I thought about the many people that I wanted to share God's love with them in Jesus

Suddenly, the whole world weighed upon my heart and soul, to a degree, that I knelt on the beach. I prayed, "Lord, I give myself to You to be used to tell others about Your love for them in Jesus."

After the prayer, I felt the burden lifted and a joy filled my heart. I knew that what I did pleased the Lord. As I walked back to my room, I thought, *the Lord wants me to serve Him in some way by using my life to tell others about Him.*

In my heart I knew the Lord was calling me out to serve Him in some special capacity. I didn't know how or when or where or what, but I knew the Lord had called me.

Later on that Sunday evening after church, I told one of the young men in the church that I thought the

Lord was calling me to serve Him in some special way. He said, "Joey, you need to get prepared. You need to go on to college and seminary. There's a group of us going to Carson-Newman College in Tennessee. You ought to go with us."

That conversation started me thinking and praying about the possibilities of going to Carson-Newman that coming fall. I got Carson-Newman's address from Bill Yoeman who was going to CNC as a freshman. I wrote Carson-Newman a letter on notebook paper and with a pencil. I didn't have the proper stationary.

In the letter I told them how I was saved and called to give my life to serve the Lord Jesus. Two weeks later, I received a reply saying that they needed my high school transcripts; I sent them the name of my high school.

The last week of August came and I had not received a reply from CNC. Bill Yoeman, and the students returning to CNC, were getting ready to go to Jefferson City, which is located thirty miles from Knoxville. I felt frustrated, because I had not received anything from CNC.

Since Bill Yoeman was going to Carson-Newman by Greyhound bus, he was anxious for me to go with him. The other students were going by car. He approached me after church on Sunday morning. "Joey, are you going to Carson-Newman, or not? I'm leaving by bus on Tuesday, and I sure hope you'll go with me."

"I don't know, Bill; I haven't heard from Carson-Newman, and I don't know what to do. I'll let you know what I'm going to do after church this evening, okay?"

Sunday afternoon I walked out to Spa Beach and paced up and down the beach. As I walked, I prayed,

"Lord, I don't know what to do. You promised that if we ask, seek and knock that you will answer. Help me to know what to do, Lord. I need to know by this evening."

Before I left the beach, I felt a rightness in my heart about going on to Carson-Newman. I didn't have any doubts about it. That evening after the church service I told Bill, "I'm going with you. I'll get my ticket tomorrow and see you at the station at one thirty on Tuesday."

Bill Yeoman and I spent the rest of Tuesday afternoon and night on the bus and arrived in Jefferson City, Tennessee at ten o'clock Wednesday morning. Two students, John I. Smith and Dal Shealy, met us at the bus station in an old jalopy. They played football for Carson-Newman; both of them stood strong for Christ and took opportunities to serve others.

John I.Smith later attended Southwestern Baptist Theological Seminary with me in Ft. Worth and became a faithful pastor. Dal Shealy became a successful football coach who coached at Carson-Newman, Baylor and Auburn.

John and Dal took us to the administration building, where Bill Yeoman was expected, and they quickly checked him in and sent him to his dormitory. Turning to me, one of the administrative assistants asked, "Tell me your name again?"

After telling her my name, she said, "When did you correspond with us? I can't seem to find a reference on you."

Upon receiving the information, she disappeared for ten minutes. Returning she said to me, "I'm sorry but we haven't received your transcripts. You'll have to come back in January."

I was alarmed and desperate. "I can't go back again. This is where God wants me."

Several of the assistants gave me a long look and then looked at one another. One of them said, "We'll talk this over and be back in a few minutes."

After several minutes passed, the assistants came out of their conference. One of them said, "You can stay in the transit room over at The Barn until the registration is over. If we hear from your school in Texas, you'll stand a chance to be enrolled. If not, you'll have to come back in January."

At least I got my foot in the door. Every morning and afternoon, I checked with the administrators about whether my transcripts had come or not. While I was in the administration office, I shared with them about my conversion, calling and my desire to attend Carson-Newman. They began to pull for me to make it.

On the morning, of the last day that I could be enrolled, I checked once more with the office, and they told me that they had not received any word from my school in Texas. One of the administrators said, "You can come back in January. By then we should have all we need."

I was sad, for in the week that I had been on campus, I had made some new friends. The fellowship with those who shared a similar calling and commitment was exhilarating. I didn't want to leave, but I would have to leave the campus and find a job.

Returning to my room, I packed my suitcase and sat down on the edge of the bed. Yes, I would leave and go to Knoxville and get a construction job and work until January, than I would come back to Carson-Newman.

While I was thinking of my next move, someone tapped on my door. It was a runner from the administration building. He blurted out, "They want to see you over there!"

I sensed that something had happened, so I raced over to the administration offices. The secretaries met me with class cards in hand. "We got your transcripts and you've been accepted. Now take these cards and hurry to get signed up for your classes. You've only got a few minutes."

They pointed me to the first classroom, and I ran over to it. I was able to sign up for every class that I was supposed to take. Two professors told me that I was fortunate to catch them, since they had planned on leaving ten minutes before I arrived.

When I had a signature on every card, I ran back to the admissions office and laid my class cards on the counter. One of the secretaries said, "No, you're to take them into Dr. Sloan's office. He's the treasurer."

When she mentioned treasurer, I knew I might be in trouble, for I only had five dollars left from my summer's money. I hurried in to Dr. Sloan's office and laid my cards on his desk. He was just about to leave for lunch, when I rushed into his office, so he was a bit irritated.

He growled at me, "How did you get these cards signed by teachers without my signature on them first?"

"I'm sorry sir. I didn't know that you had to sign them first."

"Well," he said, "How much do you want to pay?"

"Sir, I only have five dollars."

He stared at me with a look of disbelief on his face. When he noticed that I was older than the average freshman, he asked, "Have you been in the Armed Forces?"

"Yes sir. United States Marines."

"No problem. Fill out this form and give it to the secretary. You can go to school on the GI Bill."

The Lord's hand opened the way for me to enter Carson-Newman. My enrollment was not the usual way of enrolling in a college, but God works things out His way. Praise His name!

College Years

I stayed in The Barn because it was the least expensive dormitory. After getting my room assignment, I took my suitcase and went into the room. A young man was sitting at a desk, head down, reading his Bible or praying. I couldn't tell which. He was so absorbed in his endeavor that he didn't hear me come in. A plague over his desk read:

"I have only one life; t'will soon be past; only what is done for Christ will last."

In that brief moment, I was impacted by those words. I whispered a prayer: *Lord, help me to count for You.*

Charles Stirman looked up, and I introduced myself. Charles was an intense, red-headed, eighteen-years-old from Miami.

Charles and I hit it off great. We went to the same small mission church and did some jails ministries on Saturday afternoon. One day an English professor saw us walking by, and he remarked to us, "Stirman and Turman, you want to save the whole world?"

It occurred to me that we did. I replied, "You're right sir, we do."

In the middle of February, a flu epidemic hit our campus. One morning I woke up with a splitting headache, and as the day went by, I became sicker. Throughout the night, my fever raged, and I woke up the next morning so weak that I could hardly get out of bed.

I was so sick that I didn't know when they took me to the infirmary. They gave me penicillin and other medicines to control my fever. In a few days I was up and back in class.

In early April, some upper classmen from the Ministerial Association approached me on the campus. They said, "We have the program for chapel next Tuesday. Would you give your testimony?"

Without much thought, I said, "Yes, I will."

After they walked away, I felt startled by my saying yes. *Why did I say yes. To speak in chapel is a big deal and I don't know whether I can do it or not.*

The next week I spent more time in prayer than usual and more time wrestling with what I was going to say. I came to this basic conclusion: Just tell what happened to you in the clearest and best way possible and give God the glory.

The day of the chapel program arrived, and I stood off stage with the other student who was going to give his testimony. He was Tony Gonzales who came from Cuba. Tony was going to give his testimony and sing a special.

Tony and I gave our testimonies, and he sang his special. Even though I had no public speaking experience to discern the audience's response, I could tell that they were impacted by the testimonies. The Ministerial Association asked us to give our testimonies again in chapel for the upper classmen.

That experience gave me more confidence in my public speaking. After speaking in chapel, I received a number of invitations to speak in churches and before youth groups.

Called to Pastor a Mountain Church

At the end of my sophomore year, a fellow student, John Chalmers, who pastored two missions in Jamestown, Tennessee, approached me about preaching for him. He said, "I'm leaving Carson-Newman, and I need someone to take my place. Would you go down this weekend and preach in view of a call?"

I agreed to go that coming weekend. John said that he couldn't go with me, so he drew me a detail map of how to get to the Round Mountain Community, which was located on the edge of the town of Jamestown. He said, "You'll be staying with the Winningham family."

John's map was accurate, and I arrived around four o'clock that Saturday afternoon. Sister Delcie Winningham,who worked at the local hospital, met me. When I drove up to the house, she was sitting in a rocking chair on the front porch. Brother Jason, her husband, who was a farmer, was not home yet. Opal, the daughter in her thirties, appeared briefly to say hello and returned to cooking supper. Charles, the youngest in his early twenties, worked away from home.

Sister Delcie, in her early fifties, had jet black hair and matching black eyes that looked straight at you while listening or talking with you. She immediately began calling me "Brother Joey." She told me about the Round Mountain Baptist Mission: "We meet in an old school house. It's not much, but it's all we have at the present time. Brother Joey, I'm praying that someday we will have our own building and become an organized church."

About an hour later, Brother Jason came in from milking the cows. He was in his middle fifties with a ruddy, reddish complexion that spoke of his Scottish ancestry. He was not tall or heavy built, but I could see his muscled arms that gave evidence of his farm labors. His frank, open-face gaze reminded me of Jesus description of Phillip "in whom there is no guile." Brother Jason was a deacon in the church.

Opal interrupted our conversation, on the front porch, to call us to eat supper. I was hungry and enjoyed her hot biscuits, creamed potatoes, green beans and fried chicken.

The Winninghams lived simple lives. Their main literature was the Bible and related materials. Their outside news of the world came from the radio. Going to bed time was early, and getting up time was early. It was not so much of a shock to me, for I was used to farm life.

I preached at two missions each Sunday: Round Mountain and Pine Haven mission churches. That first Sunday I preached at Round Mountain, during the Sunday School hour; then I jumped into my car and drove through Jamestown to the Pine Haven Baptist Mission, to preach there at eleven o'clock. On Sunday evenings I reversed the schedule.

After the evening service at Round Mountain, I drove back to Jefferson City. John Chalmers stopped me on the campus Wednesday afternoon. "Joey, the two missions in Jamestown called me last night. They want you to come as their pastor. What do you think about it?"

"I've already prayed and thought about it. I'll be glad to be their pastor."

"Great, I'll call them tonight and tell them that you'll be there Saturday evening, okay?"

'Okay, I'll be there between three and four."

During that time, I had classes until noon on Saturdays at Carson-Newman. After a quick lunch, I packed up and headed to Jamestown. It was a hundred and twenty mile drive.

By the time I arrived at the Winninghams, the day was about over; so, I did most of my visiting on Sunday afternoons.

I enjoyed visiting the people out in the community. When I got the name of the prospects, I visited them. Some were prospects for salvation, so I shared the Gospel with them. One of them was Joe Fowler. Joe was a six-foot-three veteran of the Korean War. His wife, Charlene, was active in our church and brought the three daughters each Sunday.

One Sunday afternoon, I shared with Joe and urged him to get his life right with God. I asked him, "Joe, have you nailed down eternal life in Jesus?"

"No, I haven't."

"Does it cause you some worry and concern?"

"Yeah, I guess it does."

"Wouldn't it be better if you had that settled now, and you wouldn't have to worry about it anymore?"

"Yeah, it would."

"Why don't we do that now."

I led Joe to pray and to commit his life to Jesus as Lord and Savior. Two Sundays later, I baptized him in the baptism pool of the First Baptist Church. He was the first person I ever baptized, and I dropped him. I failed to give enough leverage, for bringing his six-foot-three frame down to the water, so he hit the water with a "kerplash." But he went under and came up sputtering.

When the summer break came, I moved in with the Winninghams and stayed with them until classes opened in September. That summer I learned the basics of being a pastor. I taught in Vacation Bible School, organized a tent revival and visited every prospect for our church in our community.

Brother Jason and Sister Delcie accepted me as a son and treated me as one of the family. I found that out in an unexpected way. One day, I went to Chattanooga to hear the Evangelist Hyman Appleman preach. I returned around one o'clock in the morning. Since I came in so late, I anticipated sleeping in; however, at six o'clock Brother Jason kept knocking on my door, until I got up and joined them for breakfast.

Then I knew that I really was going to be treated as a son. All the family got up early, and if I was going to be a part of the family, then I would need to get up and eat with the family. No lounging in bed until ten in the morning, even if I came in at one o'clock in the morning.

We had a tent revival that was an exciting experience for me and the church. I went with Joe Fowler to Livingston, a small town some twenty miles from Jamestown, to pick up a tent at the association office.

We erected the tent on the old school yard. Erecting the tent was more of a job than I thought it would be. Joe and I struggled with it for several hours, than some of the men from the church joined us, when they got off work. The opportunity to work with the men in the church helped me to get to know them.

Our next trip was to the saw mill to get a truck full of saw dust to scatter on the ground floor of the tent. How can you hit the saw dust trail without saw dust?

Our evangelist was Thad Dowdle from North Carolina. Thad had just graduated from Carson-Newman and was the pastor of a church in Franklin, NC. He was a dynamic preacher who had served as a part-time auctioneer in his late teens. When he started preaching, the words flowed out of his mouth. He was biblical, and he knew how to hold the attention of the congregation.

The tent was packed out the first night and every night afterwards. The revival started on Sunday night and went through Wednesday night. There were a number of commitments, and some came to profess Christ as Savior.

On the third night of the revival, Thad preached on John 3:3, "You Must Be Born Again."

One of the ladies down the mountain from the church, had attended every night. She did not attend our church, or probably not any church. She drove a nice car and dressed in nice looking clothes and said "amen" during the special music. But in the middle of Thad's sermon, she stood up and stalked out of the tent.

The lady started her car, raced the motor, and tore around the tent blowing her horn, over and over again. I've never seen anything like it since that time. Thad latter said to me, "I believe she let the devil take over."

Years later, even until today, people in the Round Mountain Community still talk about that tent revival meeting.

Thad Dowdle later on went to New Orleans Seminary and received his doctor's degree. He became the pastor of several large churches. He recently retired after serving for many years as a professor and then as Dean of Students, at Fruitland Bible College in Hendersonville, NC.

Charlie's Death

I lived in a rooming house off campus with three of my friends. I had a large room by myself, and the three friends had rooms across the hall from my room.

Our landlady, Miss Forrest, was a kind, Christian spinster. Even though she was in her early eighties, she drove about town and participated in church and civic activities. She had a sharp mind and enjoyed discussions.

One Sunday evening, in early November, I had arrived from serving in the churches in Jamestown. When I started to go upstairs to my room, Miss Forrest called to me. "Joey, Joey, I've got to tell you something that I don't want to tell you."

The tone of her voice and the intensity in which she spoke startled me. "Yes, Miss Forrest, is something wrong?"

"Yes, I received a telephone call from the college office," she paused, "they said that your brother, Charlie, was killed in a car accident."

She came over and took my hands. In the faint hall light, I could see tears glistening as they trickled down her cheeks. "I'm so sorry, so sad for you and your family."

I was stunned and shocked by the news. *Charlie, Charlie so virile and full of life, so handsome and quick to laugh and so generous. Charlie, dead, I can't believe it. Charlie who loved his wife and three children so much, and us, his brothers and sisters and Mama and Papa. Now he's gone.*

Standing on the stairway half-dazed, I heard Miss Forrest say, "Joey, are you all right? Can I do something?"

"No, Miss Forrest, I'll be all right. I'm going on to my room to try to get some rest. Tomorrow's going to be a busy day for me. Good night and thanks for caring."

Even though I was tired, I couldn't sleep. Charlie, my brother Charlie dead. I can't believe it. He was the brother who liked to snuggle us younger ones He had a fun-loving disposition, and his laughter was loud and spontaneous. Charlie had thick, black hair and even white teeth. He was handsome.

Early the next morning, I used Miss Forest's telephone to call the airport and make reservations for a flight to Texas. The flight left at eleven o'clock that morning. I parked my car at the airport.

When I arrived at the airport in Tyler, Buddy, my brother, met me. Upon leaving the airport, we rode several miles in silence. Buddy said, "You know how Charlie liked to drive fast. He was driving too fast and slid off the pavement and hit the gravel on the side of the road. It flipped him over and` broke his neck."

I didn't know what to say. I finally said, "It's sad. He leaves three kids."

Charlie's funeral was held at the church that his family attended in Tyler. A large crowd attended the service, for Charlie was a friendly, likeable person.

The most dramatic happening occurred during the last viewing, after the sermon. Just when the pastor announced that the family would have the opportunity for a brief last viewing, Uncle Tom Jones, our great uncle on my Papa's side, came lurching down the aisle. Every eye was riveted on him. He stood well over six feet. He looked; like a prophet, from the Old Testament, with his white hair and beard.

Uncle Tom's peg leg accentuated his unusual appearance. He was in his middle eighties, but stood straight as an arrow.

He stood by the coffin and wept. There was hardly a dry eye in the church after Uncle Tom's show of love for Charlie.

The next morning I caught my scheduled flight back to Knoxville. My heart was sad, but I knew I needed to get on with my life and mission.

A Vision Realized

Later, in Round Mountain, I was sitting on the front porch in a rocking chair talking with Sister Delcie. She communicated her vision to me. She said, "Brother Joey, I want you to pray with me about us organizing our own church and getting our own building. You know we've been meeting in that old school house for ten years, or more."

"Yeah, I will Sister Delcie. Do we have any land to put a building on?"

"No, we don't. We need to pray about that too."

Three days later, I was at Victor Garret's little country store drinking a cold drink, when Victor came in. Victor owned hundreds of acres of land, a saw mill and other enterprises. He was considered a wealthy man in that area. He was a member and deacon at the First Baptist Church in Jamestown.

After greeting Victor, I asked him, "Victor, do you know where we can buy land to build our church on? Our folks want to build our own building."

"I don't know where you can buy land, but I know where you can get some land."

That was a strange answer. I asked him, "Where?"

"I'll give Round Mountain Mission enough land to build a church on. I know just the place for the church. I'll give you two acres on the curve just before you get to the old school building. That's a great place for a church."

"You will give us the land?"

"Yeah, you tell Jason and Everett Dalton to come down to my place, and I'll make out a deed to the land for the church."

I couldn't believe it! I left the store floating on the air of praise. Praise the Lord! Prayers had been answered. I hadn't had time to pray much about it, but Sister Delcie and others in the church, had been praying for years for a building. Now, God was bringing it to past.

When I drove up to the Winningham's house, Sister Delcie was sitting in her rocking chair on the front porch. I tried to remain calm. "Sister Delcie, guess what Victor Garrett just told me?"

"What, Brother Joey?"

"He said he was going to give the church two acres of land on the curve just before the school house."

Sister Delcie stared at me to see if she heard correct. "Victor is going to give us land?"

"Yes, he said two acres on the curve."

Delcie rocked for several seconds looking out across the field in front of the house. "Brother Joey, that means we can build our own building. We have our men in the church who can do it. Joe Fowler's an electrician, Everett can lay brick, Jason's a good carpenter, and there are other men who can help out, also."

I said, "Yeah, we can do it. You know we need to organize into a church first. We've been a mission from First Baptist long enough. They've helped us, but it's time we formed our own congregation."

"Brother Joey, you talk to the men about that. I believe the Lord's in this."

Brother Jason and Brother Everett went to Victor's house and got the deed for the church property. They told me to see Dr. Alexander, the pastor of the First Baptist Church at Jamestown, about our becoming a church. They were our sponsoring church.

Dr. Alexander was happy to hear about our decision to become a church. He said, "A week from

Sunday, I'll organize the service at the First Baptist and I'll invite the Association Missionary to come and speak."

The service for organizing the Round Mountain into a constituted church went well. I took the opportunity to baptize some new converts in the baptismal pool at the First Baptist, during the early part of the service.

By the time we cleared off the land and got our building materials together, it was already the middle of September. I had returned to my classes at Carson-Newman. Every Saturday, I left Carson-Newman, as soon as I could get out of my eleven o'clock class, and drove on to Round Mountain to help with the church building.

The men started working to build the building on Saturday morning, and I joined them in the middle of Saturday afternoon. It took a while to get the foundation laid. By that time, it was already the middle of November, and the weather turned cold. The cold weather and rain delayed the building until spring.

All of the men in our church had other jobs and could only give some time on the church on Saturdays. Some Saturdays the weather was bad, and sometimes some of the men had other things they had to do on Saturday. Thus, the work on the church went slowly, albeit going forward.

But finally, the church building was completed, and we had a glorious dedication service with pot luck dinner and many guests. Many prayers went into the building of that physical building, and many prayers went into the building up of the spiritual body of Christ.

Round Mountain Baptist Church is still a thriving rural church today. The leaders in the church now were children, when I walked the hills and valleys at Round Mountain.

Visiting a Real Hero

Pine Haven Baptist Church was near Wolf River, where Sgt. Alvin York lived. I had heard many things about the World War 1 hero and his exploits in winning the Medal of Honor in the Argonne Forest. I wanted to meet him.

I asked some members of the church, "Do you think I can meet Sgt. York?"

Most of them said the same thing. "Sure, you can. He's a friendly man and likes to have visitors."

One thing I noticed about the people in Fentress County. They were proud of Sgt. York, but they thought of him as being a neighbor, a farmer like so many of them. They didn't treat him as a celebrity, as did many tourists, who looked upon him in awe.

Sgt. York was not only a hero because of his courageous exploits in the war, he was also a hero, because of what he did after the war. He refused to use his position, as a hero, to personally gain wealth. He turned down movie and business offers by the dozens.

He returned to Wolf River to marry his sweetheart and to work on his farm; however, it was not possible for him to live the normal life of a farmer. He was a hero known all over the world, and many people came to visit with him.

He had seen other countries and met people from many states and countries. His many experiences had broadened him, and he saw the need for children and young people in Fentress County to get a better education than he had received. The more he thought about it, the more he felt the need to do something about it.

Sgt York decided to build a school to accommodate the education of children and young people in his county. He was willing to use his hero status to raise money for the purpose of building a school facility.

He began traveling about Tennessee and other states speaking about the need for a school, for the children in the mountains of East Tennessee. The money began to pour in, and he collected enough to build York Academy. The school still serves the youth of Fentress County.

When Hitler, and the Third Reich, began to invade their neighboring countries and to threaten England, the United States began to prepare for war. There were those who said the war in Europe was none of our business, and we should keep out of it. At that time, the isolationist movement was strong in the nation.

Sgt. York was an interventionist. He strongly believed that we should help England with war materials, and that we should start training as many soldiers as possible for war.

So when Mr. Laskey, a movie producer from Hollywood, began to talk with Sgt. York about making a patriotic film that would inspire Americans to fight for a free world, he listened and was willing to let his story be told on film. Gary Cooper was chosen to play Sgt. York, and the film, *Sergeant York*, became a successful hit across the nation.

One day I decided to visit Sgt. York. I wanted someone to go with me, but everyone that I asked was busy; so, I went alone to the York house. Two large trees sheltered the front of the house and formed a leafy archway.

When I knocked on the door, Ms. Gracie, Sgt. York's wife, came to the door. She smiled and said, "Won't you come in?"

I said, "Thank you. I'm Joe Turman, the pastor of Pine Haven Baptist Church. I would like to meet Sgt. York and to read the Bible and pray with him."

"I'm sure he'll be glad to meet you. You come on back here. The Sergeant is sorta bedridden, but he'll be glad to visit with you."

We went back to the room, where Sgt. York was propped up on his bed. He had a comforter draped across his waist. His hair was thin and gray, and his complexion was pale. I could tell that he had not been out in the sunshine for a while.

Ms. Gracie introduced me to the Sergeant. He said, "Pull up a chair and visit awhile."

I said, "I've heard a lot about you, and I've always appreciated what you mean to our country."

"I did what I could when I had too." Then he changed the subject. "So you're a preacher at Pine Haven? That's a fine little church. Where'd you come from?"

"I'm a Texan, and I'm a student at Carson-Newman College at Jefferson City"

"That's a fine school. Yup, a good one."

"Before I was called to preach, I did a tour in the Marines. I served as an ordnance man, and I like guns."

When I mentioned guns, the Sergeant lit up. We talked about guns for the next fifteen minutes. He had a collection of guns that he wanted to show me another time.

I could see that I shouldn't stay too long. "Sergeant, I've got to go. May I read the Scripture and pray with you before I go?"

"I sure want you too. You go ahead."

I read from the Psalms and prayed for the Sergeant and his family. At the door, I said, "I'd like to come back again sometimes to visit you."

"Son, you come anytime. I enjoyed having you."

I did come back one other time to visit and to pray with the Sergeant. On another occasion when Papa, Mama and my older brother, Dan, and his family, came to visit me, I took them to visit Sgt. York. Papa had served in the Army in World War 1, so he and Sgt. York had an exciting time talking about the war. It was hard to get Papa back in the car.

Sgt. York died four years later in 1964. At that time, I was a student at the seminary in Ft. Worth, Texas. When I heard the news of the Sergeant's death, I knew that we had lost one of our greatest heroes.

In 1989, Gloria and I were invited to speak at a large church in Nashville. Joey and Anne-Marie, our two oldest children, were students at Samford University in Birmingham. They came up on a Saturday to visit with us. While we were together, we went sight-seeing in downtown Nashville. When we came outside the capitol building, we came upon the bronze stature of Sgt. York.

I didn't know the stature of the Sergeant was there. For a moment I was shocked and moved. I said to my family, "Just a few years ago I visited Sergeant York and had Bible study and prayer with him. He's one of my favorite heroes."

Joey, asked, "Dad, you knew Sgt. York and visited with him?"

"Yes, I did and I'll never forget it. He was a real hero."

Time of Transition

I graduated from Carson-Newman in January 1961. Shortly after my graduation, I was approached about serving as Youth For Christ Director for the city of Clarksville, Tennessee. I felt led to do so, but I continued to fill in at Round Mountain two times a month. Soon, it became too much for me, so I had to give up going back and forth to Jamestown.

The Youth for Christ ministry was directed toward junior high and high school students. Bible studies took place during the week and rallies on Saturday night. Between fifty and sixty young people participated in the program in Clarksville. On Saturday night the attendance often was over a hundred.

During the week, I often spoke in schools and other community events. Another opportunity for witnessing was serving through the Christian Service Men's Center. Harold Witmer, the Director, invited me to join them after the Youth for Christ's Saturday night rally, to witness to the soldiers who came into the center for a snack and a place to relax.

Sharing with the soldiers proved to be a life changing experience for many of them. On late Saturday nights, two or three of us workers from the center would go out on the streets and invite soldiers to visit the Center to get a cup of coffee and doughnuts. Many accepted our invitation and came to the Center. There, Christian soldiers shared the Good News of Christ with them. A number of soldiers have been converted and have become outstanding Christian leaders.

I was blessed and challenged through my witnessing experiences in Clarksville, but I knew my time in Clarksville would be a transitory experience. I planned on going to Southwestern Seminary in Fort Worth, Texas, as soon as I could manage to enroll. Thus, in early December, when my brother Chet called from Texas, and offered me a job selling for his franchise, I decided to go to Texas. Chet said, "Joe, you can make enough money to put yourself through the seminary."

Chet's proposition appealed to me, so I left Clarksville and went to Monroe, LA to join my youngest brother, Nick, in getting started on my new job.

I arrived in Monroe, Louisiana at one o'clock in the morning and went to the hotel that Chet had suggested to me. I took a small handbag with my shaving gear, and I left most of my clothes hanging in the back of the car. That was a mistake, for during the night, someone broke into the car and stole some of my best clothes.

My youngest brother, Nick, greeted me in time for a cup of coffee and breakfast. He was to help me get started in my new job. Nick, tall, Hollywood good-looking and laid back was a lot of fun to work with in selling. He was one of the best salesmen in the franchise.

Later on in the day, he took me out to a neighborhood to follow up on leads made by the telephone ladies. Calls were made from our office in the hotel to offer five popular magazines at a fantastic bargain. Those, who were magazine readers, were interested, and many said yes to the deal. A sales order was written up by the telemarketer, and we salesmen went out to close the deal.

Nick had a handful of leads. "Josephus," he said, "You just watch how I do it."

Nick drove up to the first house. He motioned for me to go with him to the door. He was at ease, like he was going up to a friend's house. He knocked on the door with a loud firm knock.

A housewife came to the door. "Hello ma'm, I'm Nick Turman from the Keystone Reader's Club. Our secretary called you earlier, and I'm here to help you with your selection of magazines. May I step in for a moment."

In five minutes or less, Nick had the order and the payment for the first month of magazines. He closed seven out of eight leads in rapid succession. "See Joseph," he said, "It aint hard to do, is it?"

I was excited. "It looks easy enough."

"Let's go get some lunch, and after lunch we'll go by the office and get some new leads. Then I'm gonna turn you loose."

We drove up to the house for my first lead. Nick said, "Joseph, I'm gonna stay in the car. Just go up to that door like you're the most important man in this town who has something you want to share with her…or him."

I bounded up to the door and pounded on it, probably harder than Nick. Before I could step back, a man opened the door. "Whatta ya want?" he growled.

My throat constricted and my voice came out raspy and squeaky. "I'm…I'm Joe Turman from the Keystone Reader's Club. And…and… we called and someone here said they would like some of our magazines."

"Honey," the man called over his shoulder, "Did you order some magazines?"

"No, I didn't"

The man glared at me. "We don't want any."

He slammed the door. *That lady lied. She did order magazines.*

When I came back to the car, Nick smiled at me. He had watched and heard the conversation. "Don't worry Joseph. In some cases like this when the man is at home, the wife won't admit that she agreed to an order. Now men are actually easier to sell than women. If I can get in and talk to them for a few minutes, I'll sell the men."

At my next house, the lady was waiting for someone to show up and get her order. That order gave me some confidence in making my next calls. As the days went by, I became more and more at ease in closing out orders. Nick said to me, "Joseph, you're getting plumb good."

One morning I ate breakfast in a restaurant down the street from the hotel. Nick skipped breakfast for a cup of coffee. When I came back to the hotel, I told Nick about my experience at breakfast: "You know one of the waitresses was real friendly. She told me that her mom is about to die, but she doesn't have enough money to go home to see her. Sorta sad…"

Nick laughed. "How much did you give her, Josefus?"

I was somewhat startled. "Well, I gave her twenty."

"Last week I gave her twenty to go to see her dying mother. Brother Joe, we've been taken. No problem for she probably needs it."

That was Nick, easy going, generous and willing to cut some slack for others along the way.

One morning at breakfast, Nick said, "Whitey's coming today."

"Who's Whitey?"

"He's the franchise owner's older brother."

"Is he coming to check up on us?"

Nick drained his coffee cup. "Naw, he's coming to play around. You'll like Whitey. He's not like his brother. His brother's all business, but Whitey, well Whitey likes to have a good time. He's an old magazine salesman who has a ton of stories. He sorta works as his brother's sales manager."

Around one o'clock Whitey showed up at the office. He and Nick evidently were already good friends. He shook hands with me. "Well, Joe. I've already heard that you can close 'em out. Let's go get a cup of coffee, and I've got a few things I wanna tell you that'll help you to be the super salesman that you're gonna be."

Two hours and four cups of coffee later, we came back to the office. Whitey was just getting warmed up, but Nick seized up the situation. "Whitey, we gotta let Joe get out there and close the rest of these leads. We've got something we need to do, remember?"

"Yeah, you're right, Nick. Hey Joe, Nick and I are going to find a Studebaker. I hear they got one over in Bastrop. Don't wait up for us, hear?"

I went about my work. *They're gone to find a Studebaker? They stop producing Studebakers twenty years ago.*

Nick and Whitey went to search for a Studebaker several more times. They knew that I didn't drink or carouse around in nightclubs, so that was their polite way of telling me that they were going out to do their thing. I didn't need to know where they went or what they did.

While Whitey was in town, we did very little work. We went bowling, shot pool and told stories. I might say Whitey did most of the story telling. His stories were funny, but not dirty.

Whitey was like someone who stepped out of a Damon Runyon story. He could enchant you with his charm and story- telling. He could care less about the volume of sales. He wanted to be around people and entertain them with his stories.

Even though I spent six months working as a salesman, I made very little money, but I gained a ton of new experiences that would last me through life. Now a new chapter was about to begin in my life.

Going to the Seminary

In the time of my working as a salesman, I made only enough money to get by on, with a little left over. The last week in August, I went to Ft. Worth and enrolled at Southwestern Baptist Theological Seminary. I found out that the cost of enrollment was not so costly and that my main expense would be for my dorm room and food.

I figured that I could get a part-time job to pay for my room and food. Since I had experience selling magazines, I checked in with the Ft. Worth branch of Keystone Readers.

Vernon Bradford was the manager. He was an easy-going, heavy set man who had started selling magazines from door to door. Now he drove a large black Lincoln and enjoyed a degree of prosperity. He was pleased to meet me and to know of my experience in selling.

I sat in his office for an hour talking with him about mutual acquaintances in the magazine business and sharing our experiences in selling. After a while, he said, "Joey, how about going out and closing some leads for me? I'll take you in my car. You can have all the down payments you can get."

When we drove up to a house in Vernon's big, black limo, I swaggered up to the door full of confidence. How could I not be confident? A big black, shiny limo, driver and someone watching who thought I was a selling whiz. I closed out all of his leads that afternoon without missing a beat. The next day, Vernon took some new salesmen with us, so they could watch me close out leads. Fortunately, the leads were in solid neighborhoods, where those who ordered them, really wanted magazines for a good price. I closed out all but two of the leads.

One day, I attended the Salvation Army Mission meeting in downtown Ft. Worth. The man who brought the message was Brother Tom Kellam. After the service, I had the occasion to meet and talk with him. I found out that he had graduated from Southwestern Seminary back in the fifties, when he was in his middle thirties.

He had been saved from a drunkard's life. After his dramatic conversion, he came to the seminary and got his diploma degree. He felt called to travel the states and preach in the downtown rescue missions. He had been in all the well-known missions from Chicago, New York and to numerous other cities.

He reminded me of Santa Clause, with his silver grey hair, twinkling blue eyes, round cherry-colored complexion and big friendly smile.

One day, Brother Tom asked me, "Joey, how about you working with me in these missions? We can take turns in preaching, okay?"

"Okay, but sometimes I'll be unable too because of my studies."

"That's all right. Whenever you can. I've been in the seminary and I know what it's like."

So Brother Tom and I hit it off from the beginning and became good friends. We would often eat together at Lavender's Cafeteria, which was located near the seminary. It was the best priced cafeteria in Ft. Worth, and you could eat all you wanted. On some days I would have only a cup of coffee for breakfast and put it on at Lavender's at noon. Brother Tom did the same, and so did many students, who were struggling to make ends meet.

It was no surprise that Lavender's soon went out of business. We sorely missed the good food and prices.

Even though I did well, when I closed out leads for Keystone Readers, I only worked one or two afternoons a week. I still barely made enough to make it through the week.

I made an effort to find another job, but most of the jobs were already taken by students.

My study load at the seminary was not heavy, but it was enough to keep my nose in the books. I wanted to be equipped to go out as a pastor/ evangelist, so I had a desire to use my time, while in the seminary, to be prepared for a wider and deeper ministry.

One day, Brother Tom Kellum said to me, "Joey, I want you to visit the zoo with me. I've got something I want to show you. You'll be surprised."

Believe me, I was surprised when I went to the zoo.

Racing the Gorilla

Brother Tom liked zoos. He said, "In every city I go too, I visit the zoos and become acquainted with the animals. I know most of the animals by their names. The zoo workers tell me the names of the animals."

I was curious and could hardly wait to visit the zoo with Brother Tom. At the agreed time, I met Brother Tom downtown, and we drove to the zoo. He directed me to park inside the zoo near the cage of the gorillas.

We got out of the car, and as we walked to the gorilla cage, he said, "Joey, the big gorilla in this cage is named Mike. Mike and I are friends, and he likes to race me."

"He likes to race you? I don't believe it."

"Well, you watch and see."

When we walked up to the cage, Mike was pouting in a corner of the cage. Some zoo visitor had insulted him. Brother Tom approached the cage and called out in a moderate voice, "Mike, hey Mike, I've come to visit and race you."

Mike glanced over his shoulder and when he saw it was Brother Tom, he came over to the edge of the cage and got in a runner's crouch. Brother Tom got in his runner's stance outside the cage and counted off; "One, two, three, go!"

They raced to the other end of the cage and then raced back. Mike won the race.

Brother Tom explained, "I have to let Mike win the race. If I win, he pouts and won't race anymore with me."

I was excited. "Do you think Mike will race me?"

"Yeah, he might. You get down in your stance and I'll call him over."

I got down in my runner stance and Brother Tom called Mike to come and race me. Mike looked me over carefully, but with Brother Tom's coaxing he came over and got in his runner's position. He raced me to the end of the cage and back.

Several afternoons later, I was in Vernon's office picking up some leads to close out. I said to Vernon, "A few days ago, I went to the zoo with a friend of mine and watched him race a gorilla. I've never seen anything like it. He even raced me."

What I said really caught Vernon's attention. "You're kidding me? Race a gorilla, I don't believe it."

"I didn't either, but I saw it with my own eyes, and then I did it."

Vernon called everyone over in the office. "Hey Joey, tell 'em what you just told me. This is the funniest thing I've heard in a long time."

Before I left the office, Vernon said, "Joey, do you think the Gorilla will race me?"

"Yeah, with Brother Tom's help, I think he will."

"Joey, how about you getting Brother Tom this Friday, and we'll go get a steak and afterwards go to the zoo. How about that?"

"Sounds good, Vernon. We'll do it."

That Friday at noon, Brother Tom and I came to Vernon's office and the three of us got in his big shiny Lincoln and went to the steak house. After a delicious steak, we drove to the zoo and parked his large, black, shiny limo near Mike's cage. Both Vernon and Brother Tom had on suits and ties.

When we arrived at the cage, we had a number of zoo visitors standing around staring at Mike. Mike had his arms folded and, evidently, was not enjoying his visitors. Brother Tom spoke to Mike. "Mike, I've brought some visitors with me."

Mike unfolded his arms and came over to the edge of the cage. He was glad to see Brother Tom. Mike looked at us for a few moments, then as if to say, "Let's get on with it," he got down in his runner's stance.

Brother Tom positioned himself in his stance, and they race to the end of the cage and back. Vernon was beside himself. He kept saying, "I can't believe it. I can't believe it."

He asked Brother Tom, "Do you think he'll race me?"

"Yeah, I think he will. Give me a few seconds with Mike."

Brother Tom went to the cage's edge and talked with Mike. "Mike, I've got a friend here who wants to race you. His name is Vernon." He pointed to Vernon.

Mike didn't nod his head in affirmation, but I declare, I could tell that it was all right with him.

Vernon, in his expensive suit, got down in the runner's stance, and Mike got down in his stance. Brother Tom called out to Vernon, "Don't beat him, Vernon. Let him win."

Then Brother Tom counted for the race, "One, two, three, go!"

They raced to the end of the cage and back. By this time, a large crowd gathered to watch the drama. They applauded after the race. Vernon was so excited that he raced three more times. You could tell that Vernon and Mike bonded that afternoon.

Vernon called me into his office a few days later. I could tell that he felt uncomfortable about what he was going to say. "Joey, I don't want to do this, but I've hired three permanent salesmen, and I don't need you anymore in the afternoons. I just barely keep them with enough leads to close out."

"No problem, Vernon. I understand."

"Joey, I still want us to get together to eat out, and then go to the zoo. Do you still think we can do that?"

"Vernon, it will be my pleasure to get together with you any time. Just let me know."

Vernon did call me a number of times. He took Brother Tom and I out for steak, and then we went to the zoo and raced Mike. It was always fun.

That summer I sold Bibles for The Southwestern Company of Nashville, Tennessee. A fellow seminary student, and I, sold in Northern Virginia. I made enough money to buy a VW bug, and to pay for my seminary expenses.

That year, at the seminary, I met someone who would change the course of my life.

Gloria

With some money in the bank, I enjoyed my seminary experience a lot more. I didn't have to rush out to try to sell after class, in order to get enough money to eat on.

That fall was a memorable time. On November 22, 1963, President John F. Kennedy was assassinated in Dallas. He, Jackie, and his entourage, spent the night in Ft. Worth before they went on to Dallas the next morning. He did make a speech in Ft. Worth and several seminary students went to hear him.

After a busy morning of classes, I went out to the basketball court to shoot some baskets. Someone walked by and said that President Kennedy had been shot in Dallas. I went in to the TV room in the dorm. It was already full of students. I heard Walter Cronkite tell the nation that President Kennedy was dead. It was a sad day.

That spring of 1964, I met Gloria. She had entered the seminary in September 1963, but I didn't get to know her until the last days of classes in May 1964. When finals were over, some of us students got together to go bowling. The graceful, well-built young lady that beat us all in bowling was Gloria Ann Reece.

I made a point to get to know Gloria. Her brown eyes and engaging smile attracted me. The remaining two days on campus I saw her several times and had conversations with her. I found out she was from Brownsville, Tennessee and lived on highway 70, near the town.

I said to her, "Byron Banta and I are going to Nashville to sales school. We'll be going past your house."

Gloria said, "Why don't you drop by and get some cookies and coffee to keep you awake?"

"Okay, we will. Don't be surprised when we knock on the door."

"I won't, come on by."

Byron and I arrived in Memphis around four o'clock in the afternoon. He wanted to drop by the house of a young lady he had been dating at the seminary. When we finally found her house, it was near six o'clock. The girl's family invited us to eat with them. They were having a cook out with another family, and the aroma of cooking steaks convinced us to stay.

It was around nine o'clock in the evening before we got back on Highway 70, to go through Brownsville, on the way to Nashville. By the time we arrived at Gloria's house, it was ten o'clock in the evening. Their house was located in a farming community, seven miles from Brownsville.

When we pulled into the driveway, I noticed there were no lights on in the house. I said to Byron, "They're in bed. There's no lights on in the house."

Byron said, "The shades are probably pulled down. Get up there and knock on that door, you coward."

Against my better judgment, but prodded by Byron's words, I knocked on the door. After waiting for several seconds, I turned to go when the door opened. Gloria's mother said, "Yes, what do you want?"

I stammered, "I…uh…Gloria said we could drop by for coffee."

It sounded ridiculous even to me, and I meant to say, "Please don't bother, it's late." But before I could say anything, she called out, "Gloria, somebody is here to see you."

Gloria appeared in less than a minute looking so pretty and fresh. She said, "You all come on in. Where's Byron?"

"Here's in the car. I'll get him. Maybe it's too late for us, isn't it?"

"No, it's okay. We just got in bed. I've got the cookies and coffee for you."

We enjoyed the cookies, coffee and conversation with Gloria. We apologized to Mrs. Reece for coming in so late. She didn't seem to mind.

On our way to Nashville, Byron spoke prophetically, "Joe, you're going to marry that girl."

Before leaving, I asked Gloria if we could write one another. She agreed and we traded three or four letters. That summer she worked at Ridgecrest and Glorieta, the Baptist Assemblies.

After that summer, something more serious came about.

Dating and Marriage

Back at the seminary, I began a dating relationship with Gloria. Our dating consisted of going to get a burger and coke, or going to the zoo, botanical gardens, or just window shopping.

After Christmas, I went to Brownsville to meet Gloria's family. They were hard-working farm folks who lived simple but full lives. They got up early and went to bed early.

Mr. Reece enjoyed telling stories. He could go to town on Saturday and have a half-dozen, or more, people gather around him to hear his stories. He kept up with world news, sports and could entertain almost any subject you wanted to discuss.

While there, I was invited to preach, and Mrs. Reece came to hear me. That made me a little nervous, but I think I did okay.

On the last day of the year, Gloria and I went to Memphis to bring in the New Year. She would stay with her older sister, Marilyn, and I would stay with my old Marine buddy, Jack Turner, who was now married and had two small children.

Jack approached me about the coming New Year Eve: "Hey, Joey, why don't you and Gloria come here to bring in the New Year. Billie and I have a party with old school friends and we'll put our kids to bed around eight. You and Gloria can have the house to yourself. You can watch the Orange Bowl and bring in the New Year."

Since we didn't have anything planned, we thought it was a good idea. Jack and Billie left at eight. Gloria and I raided the fridge and settled in to watch Alabama and Texas in the Orange Bowl.

At half time, I had a plan in mind. While Gloria was sitting on the couch, I took her hands, looked deep into her beautiful brown eyes, and proposed to her. “Gloria, I love you. Would you marry me?”

I don’t know whether I surprised Gloria, or not, but she said “yes.” Maybe a proposal should be longer and more eloquent, but I just said the basics. It was from the heart.

We finished the semester and were married on May 23, 1965, in Shaw’s Chapel Baptist Church. Shaw’s Chapel is a beautiful “Little church in the wildwoods” out in the country, about three miles from Gloria’s house.

We went to Paris Landing on Kentucky Lake for the first few days of our honeymoon, then on to the Smokey Mountains. Coming back from our honeymoon, we went straight to Nashville to attend sales school. After sales school, we located in Valdosta, Georgia. Billy Bob and Nancy Robinson were our associates for the summer. They were friends from the seminary and married the same day that we married.

It was a good summer of sales. Billy Bob and I left before eight o’clock and came in after eight or nine o’clock in the evening. We did not sell together, but went to different parts of the county. Gloria and Nancy did things together. They did some work with one of the churches during the day. It was a pleasant summer.

We returned to the seminary for our last year of study. Gloria would graduate with a Master of Religious Education, and I would receive a Bachelor of Divinity, which would later be upgraded to a Master of Divinity.

Gloria and I had some exciting days ahead of us at Possum Kingdom.

Pastor at Possum Kingdom

The last of September, of our last year at the seminary, we were called to be pastor and wife of a church in Graford, Texas. Lukingdom Baptist Church is located on the shores of Possum Kingdom Lake. The congregation ran around thirty to forty people on a good Sunday. We often had visitors who were spending the weekend on the lake.

Sitting near the church was the parsonage. We drove up on Saturday mornings and stayed in the parsonage until Monday morning. The inside bathrooms didn't work, so we had a "Path" instead of a "Bath."

We went along with it until we found out that the area was thickly populated with rattlesnakes. At night, we didn't go to the outdoor toilet anymore. We used a slop jar until the plumbing was taking care of.

One Sunday, something happened that underscored the wisdom of not going to the toilet at night. Gloria and I were taking a Sunday afternoon walk near the parsonage and came upon the longest and meanest looking rattlesnake I've ever seen. He must have been six feet long.

I grabbed a rock and zinged it at him and luckily hit him on the head and keeled him over. I finished him off with two more rocks. We hung him on the fence near the church, and the ole rattler attracted a number of people to stop and look him over.

One thing I wanted our congregation to do was to take a community survey. We didn't know who the prospects were in our community. The three deacons were cool to the idea. They said, "We know everybody here in this community. We don't need a survey."

I was determined to take a survey, so I said, "Well, do you mind if the young people work with me and Gloria on a weekend to take a survey? We might discover more unchurched young people here."

"Yeah, that's okay. That might work."

I knew that we would find more young people, and we would find other age groups, also. We planned and organized the survey to be on a last Saturday and Sunday of March. All the young people came out to help us, and a number of adults in the church came out, also.

In the survey, we discovered ninety-nine prospects for the church. Out of the ninety-nine prospects, we won and baptized six people, four teen-agers and two adults. It was the first baptism the church had had in the past two years.

The survey was not only a blessing to the people in the community; it was a blessing to every member who participated.

In early May, I signed up to go on Spring Revivals with seminary teams. Every spring, the seminary sponsored teams to go to one of the pioneer areas for Southern Baptist to hold revivals. Two students would compose a team. The ideal was to have a music man and a preacher. Many of the teams, like my team, ended up with two preachers.

Brother Maurice Pinkston and I were assigned to go to Shelbyville, Indiana to hold a revival meeting in the Beacon Baptist Church. Brother Maurice looked like he had stepped out of the pages of a German magazine with his stout, thick-chested build, blue eyes and blond crew cut.

Maurice was from Memphis, and he was congenial and easy to work with. We had a nice time talking together, as we drove from Ft. Worth to Shelbyville.

We arrived in Shelbyville at five o'clock in the evening. We were given a name to contact. The family would keep us in their home during our stay. We contacted the family, and they invited us to come for dinner that evening and prepare to stay with them for the week.

Corrine and Estus met us at the door and graciously helped us in with our suitcases. Estus was recuperating from a light heart attack and had been away from his job for three weeks.

The next morning Maurice and I prepared to lead in our first revival effort at the church. About thirty people were present. I led the singing and Maurice did the preaching. On Sunday night we reversed the team, as I did the preaching and Maurice led the singing. Neither one of us were musically inclined.

Frank Richards, a member, saw that we were not musicians and volunteered to lead the music. Maurice and I were grateful for Frank stepping up to lead the music program. Later on, Frank became the regular music leader for the church.

On Sunday afternoon we told the church leaders that we were going to go from door to door in the community to share the Gospel. They said, "You may be able to do that in the South, but you can't do it here. It won't work."

We were determined and confident that we could go from door to door anywhere. We said, "We'll give it a try and see how it works up here."

On Monday morning, we started knocking on doors in the community. That week the only people who came to profess Christ in the revival were the six people that we led to know Christ as a result of door to door visitation. All six followed through and were baptized.

We closed out the revival meetings on Wednesday evening. Beacon Baptist Church was stirred by the revival and had a new vision for its purpose in Shelbyville. They didn't have a pastor and asked us to pray for them in calling a pastor.

I returned to the seminary revived. In meeting other students who had held revivals in different cities and towns in Indiana, I heard stories of how God blessed and moved in their meetings.

At that time I didn't realize that God had plans for Gloria and I in Indiana.

Called to Indiana

Gloria and I continued our ministry at Lukingdom Baptist Church. We both graduated from the seminary in early May and moved our meager belongings to the parsonage.

Since I had only a Volkswagan "Bug," I borrowed my older brother Dan's car. He owned a large Chevrolet convertible that he had been trying to sell. It had a spacious back seat and a large trunk. We didn't have much to move from our small apartment in Ft. Worth, but it was too much to haul in our Volkswagan.

We moved our household goods to the parsonage and drove back to Ft. Worth to turn our apartment back to the seminary and close out other business. While there, the last evening, we went downtown to see the movie, *The Sound of Music.*

When we came out of the theater around ten o'clock, we walked a block from the theater to where we parked the Chev convertible. It wasn't where I thought I parked it. Gloria said, "Maybe it's parked in the next block."

We walked all over the area looking for the car. Finally, we came to the realization that someone had stolen the car. We walked back to the movie theater and used a phone to call the police.

A police car drove up to where we were standing in front of the theater. The driver told us to get in, and he took us to the police station. The police began to give me the third degree; they suspected that I might have had the car wrecked to get the insurance money on it.

I didn't realize at the time that Ft. Worth was the car theft capitol of the USA. Dozens of cars were stolen every day, and many of them were wrecked, so the owners could pick up insurance money on them. During the questioning, I told them that I was a seminary student. They dropped the questioning and told me that the car had been stolen and wrecked on the freeway.

I borrowed a phone at the police station and called Dan. It was already one o'clock in the morning, but I wanted Dan to know what happened. I hated to get him out of bed. "Hello Dan," I said, "I hate to call you this time of night, but someone stole your car."

"They stole my car?"

"Yeah, they stole your car. And Dan they totaled it on the freeway. I'm so sorry about that."

There were several seconds of silence. "Dan, are you still there?"

"Yeah, I'm still here. Hey, don't worry about it, okay. Things like that happen. Don't be upset about it. No big problem. Go home and get a good night's sleep."

After I hung up, I said to Gloria, "Dan is such a great guy. He just took that news in the middle of the night, and it didn't seem to bother him one bit."

Later on, I heard that Dan was able to get top dollar payment from the insurance company on the totaled Chev. That made me feel better about everything. Actually, a totaled Chev was the best scenario for Dan, for he wasn't able to sell it.

In the middle of June, Beacon Baptist Church in Shelbyville, Indiana called us to come as pastor, and wife. Gloria and I were in our comfort zone at the Lukingdom Baptist Church. The people were easy to work with and saw to it that we were taken care of materially. Almost every day, someone came by with meats and vegetables for us. There was no pressure from the church to get anything done.

We spread out the call before the Lord. Beacon was the only Southern Baptist church in Shelbyville. It ran twenty-five people in Sunday School and sometimes thirty to thirty-five for the worship service. At least three or four of the members wanted to reach out to the community. The others were members who supported the church program, but were not excited about getting outside the walls of the church.

As we prayed about going to Shelbyville, we begin to feel excitement about the possibilities of sharing the Gospel in this city of twenty-five thousand people. During the last week of June, we telephoned the church and told them we would come.

The following day, I told the chairman of the deacons, Brother Cecil, that we accepted a call from a church in Indiana. I said, "I hate to leave you all so soon, because you'll have to find another pastor."

Brother Cecil said, "Don't worry about it, Brother Joey. There's plenty of preachers around here. We can get another one with no trouble."

Brother Cecil was right. As someone said about the preacher situation in that area, "You can shake a bush and a preacher will come out."

But that was not so in Indiana. The Baptist churches in Indiana had a difficult time in getting preachers to fill their pulpit. Indiana was a pioneer area for Southern Baptist, and what Brother Cecil said only confirmed our call to go north.

We left for Indiana the second week in July with our Volkswagan bug pulling a small U-haul trailer. The church had scouted out a possible apartment for us, located beside the fair grounds. After our approval, we moved in and unpacked. Several men in the church helped us place our few belongings in the apartment.

The second week on the field, the six people who had made professions of faith in Jesus during the revival, wanted to be baptized. The seventh, an eighteen-year-old, had gone into the army and was going to Vietnam.

On a Sunday afternoon, after the worship service and lunch, the entire congregation gathered at a creek some five miles from Shelbyville to baptize the six candidates. We sang a few songs, read Scripture and baptized the six new believers. It was a grand and memorable service that is still mentioned even to this day.

Gloria and I had some surprises, testing times and blessings in the times to come.

A New Family Member and A New Step in Life

On January5th, 1968, our first child, Joseph Reece Turman, was born in the middle of an Indiana snowstorm. Mrs. Reece came up a few days before he was born to help out. Our little apartment had only one bedroom, so I slept on the living room couch. We kept vigil until Joey came kicking and yelling into the world early on the evening of January the fifth. I couldn't have been prouder.

When I went back to the apartment to grab a few hours' sleep, I put a large sign in our plate glass front window: "It's a boy!" Our neighbors were all waiting for news of the coming baby.

We had a rocking chair, and I learned how to rock Joey and feed him with his bottle. Getting up at two in the morning was new for me, but I did it some nights to give Gloria an opportunity to catch up on her rest and strength. Holding and feeding your own baby is special, and I enjoyed it.

In the spring of 1968, we finished writing our biographies for the Foreign Mission Board. We had started in January after a visiting missionary, Bob Beatty, gave us a nudge to do so. Bob, and his wife, served with the Foreign Mission Board of the SBC, in Southern Rhodesia (Now Zimbabwe). He spoke at our church in early December for the Lottie Moon Christmas Offering. After the service, he asked us, "What have you all done about foreign missions?" We both said rather proudly, "Oh, we're foreign mission volunteers."

Bob responded, "What have you done about it? Are you communicating with the Board? Have you written your life history?"

"No, so many good things are going on here that we've had no opportunity to communicate with the Board."

Bob said, "He that knows to do good and does not do it, sins."

We both recognized that Bob was paraphrasing a verse from the Book of James. It convicted us that we should get on with communicating with the mission board. By the first of June, we had finished writing our bios and sent them to the Foreign Mission Board (Now it's the International Mission Board). They invited us to attend a regional meeting for candidates interested in serving as foreign missionaries.

While attending the meeting, the mission board representative asked us where we felt led to serve. We said, "We don't know."

"Call me when you know where you feel called to serve."

In the middle of June, we went to Tennessee and left Joey with Grandma Reece and went on to Ridgecrest to attend Foreign Mission Week. Four of the speakers that week were Bob and Priscilla Compher and Walter and Pauline Routh from Vietnam. They were good speakers, and what they said grabbed our hearts.

From the moment that we heard about what God was doing in Vietnam, we knew that Vietnam was the country that we would serve in. On the way back to Brownsville, Tennessee, I asked Gloria, "If you had to say now where you felt led to serve, what would you say?"

Without any hesitation Gloria said, "Vietnam." She said, "How about you?" "Vietnam. There's no doubt, it's Vietnam."

When we arrived back in Brownsville, we didn't say anything to Mr. and Mrs. Reece about our decision to go to Vietnam. On the way Gloria had said to me, "Please don't mention this to Mom and Dad. Let me choose the time and place to tell them."

We went back to Shelbyville, but we didn't mention our commitment to go to Vietnam to the church. We had not yet been approved by the mission board. We called the representative and told him about our decision to go to Vietnam. He said, "I'll turn in your names and all your information to the board members. You'll have to be approved before we can continue processing you."

A week later, we received a call from our personnel rep and he said, "I'll call you next Tuesday about whether you're approved or not."

That Tuesday we waited all day and did not receive a call. Needless to say, we were dejected. I told Gloria, "If you're not approved, they don't call you; they write you. We ran all kinds of scenarios through our minds about why we might have been rejected. It was a terrible twenty-four hours.

After a restless night, we woke to a beautiful summer day. The phone rang around nine o'clock. The mission board rep was on the line. "I'm sorry I didn't call you yesterday. We had the death of a colleague's wife, and we all attended her funeral. You all have been approved. I'm sorry about the delay. I'll be sending you materials to get you started with the process for appointment as missionaries."

The mission representative's delay in calling us had caused a lot of stress and anxiety, but the feeling of relief and joy swept that all away. We were going to be foreign missionaries! Before the end of the week, the mission rep told us to get ready to go to Atlanta to get our physical and psychiatric examinations.

Knowing that we were going to serve as foreign missionaries gave us an expectant and excited feeling. We were eager to move ahead with the preparation.

Moving On toward Foreign Missions

The following Sunday we told our church that we were going to be appointed as missionaries, and the next Sunday would be our last Sunday with the church. We wanted to go ahead and move to Tennessee in order to spend time with Gloria's family.

I called my friend, Harold Witmer, in Clarksville and told him about our appointment, and how we needed a place to stay before we went overseas. We knew several months would be involved in getting ready to go to the mission field, and we didn't want to live with Gloria's parents for that length of time. Harold said, "I'll find you something and call you back before the day is over."

In three hours Harold called back. He said, "Mr. Barnette is going to let you use one of his apartments. It won't cost you anything."

I had met Mr. Barnette when I worked for Youth for Christ in Clarksville. He was a fine Christian businessman who expressed his faith in his every day walk and talk. He owned several businesses in Clarksville and was successful in his business ventures.

Our last Sunday at Beacon Baptist Church was a pleasant day. A surprise going away party was organized for us Sunday night after the evening service. Our leaving Beacon Baptist was not as easy, emotionally, as we thought it would be. We had developed close ties with a number of the church members.

When we looked over all that we needed to move, we didn't have that much. It was only then that we found out the church people had furnished the house from their own household goods. Frank and Thelma Richards had given their bedroom suite for the apartment, and they slept on a sleeper. Other members had given other pieces of furniture to the apartment.

We were moved by the sacrifice the Beacon Baptist Church members had made in renting and preparing a place for us to live. Frank and Thelma insisted that we take the bedroom suit with us, but we said, "No way we're going to take your bedroom suite. You've been without it for two years. We'll never forget your generosity."

We rented a small U-Haul trailer and it was sufficient to haul all of our household goods. After saying farewell, we headed for Clarksville, Tennessee. After checking in with Harold, we went to see Mr. Barnette. He was a tall, heavyset man with silver-grey hair and a quick smile. He took us to the apartment that we would live in, until the first of the coming year. He said, "If you need anything else, let me know." We knew that he meant it.

While in Clarksville we joined the Cumberland Drive Baptist Church. My friend, and fellow Carson-Newman graduate, Harold Campbell, was the pastor of the church. Harold and his wife, Sherry, also a Carson-Newman graduate, made us feel welcome. They wanted to know how they could help us prepare for overseas service. Our time at Cumberland Drive was a very pleasant time.

The Foreign Mission Board (Now IMB) sent us $800.00 for an outfit allowance. This money was for buying the things we needed to take to the field with us, like a stove, fridge, washing machine and bed head boards and mattresses.

Since Harold Witmer knew about everyone in Clarksville and how and who to go to about getting things, I asked him where should I go and who do I see to buy these household goods. He said, "Give me the list and

I'll get it done. How much money do you have to spend?"

"Eight hundred dollars," I said.

"It'll take a little time, but I'll get everything for the best price."

Harold did exactly that. He bought everything we needed, and it came out exactly $800.00. He went to stores owned and ran by people he knew and told them what he wanted was for a missionary friend going to Vietnam. He bought everything for cost, except for a fridge. He bought it for $50.00.

With the money from speaking engagements, we bought toilet paper, food supplies, and many other items needed for the running of a household. Getting all these things together, we contacted a trucking company to come and crate up everything and hold it until we notified them where to send it.

By the time we had finished buying and crating the household goods, it was two days before Christmas. Our money was gone, except for $5.00. I said to Gloria, "Let's go and spend Christmas with your folks. We'll use the $5.00 to buy gas to get to Brownsville, and while there, we can borrow enough money to get by until more money comes in.

On the way out, we stopped at our mailbox to get the mail. Gloria opened the letters as I drove. I heard her exclaim, "Look at this! You won't believe it." She held up a $100.00 check that someone sent us. God is able and provides us what we need, as we strive to do His will.

We enjoyed Christmas time with the family in Brownsville. Since Gloria was expecting soon, Mrs. Reece suggested that we come on back to Brownsville a few days after the New Year and stay with them until the baby arrived.

We thought that was a good idea, so we went back to Clarksville and packed up our few belonging, said our good-byes and returned to stay with Gloria's mom and dad. The baby was in no hurry in coming, so the time for the opening day of orientation was soon upon us.

We were under pressure to decide to stay in Brownsville until the baby comes, or to go on to missionary orientation at Ridgecrest, NC.

What were we going to do?

A New Baby and Missionary Orientation

Gloria and I decided to go on to Ridgecrest, check in for orientation and have the baby at Asheville. Mrs. Reece was not happy about that decision. She said, "You may have the baby on the way. It's not a good idea to travel when you're expecting at any time."

She probably was right, but we had been at their house for almost three weeks, and we were anxious to join the other missionaries at Ridgecrest. The Foreign Mission Board representative suggested that I could go on to orientation alone, then come back and get Gloria, Joey and the new baby later on.

We nixed that idea and decided that we would all go together. Early on the morning of the 23rd of January, 1969, we said good-bye to Gloria's parents and drove toward Western Carolina, passing Nashville and Asheville on the way. Joey, our one-year-old, was a happy camper during the trip.

Upon our arrival in Black Mountain, NC, at Ridgecrest Baptist Assembly, we were warmly greeted by David and Susie Lockard who were the orientation directors. In a short time, we met old friends from seminary days who were on the same journey. One couple, Charles and Barbara Cole, were expecting their second child in a matter of weeks.

We soon were caught up in the camaraderie of being with those of similar age and mission in life. It was an exhilarating time.

On the third day of orientation, I had been invited to join several fellow missionaries to work with a church in a witnessing venture. Later on, around five o'clock we arrived back at the orientation center. Several anxious people met me and told me that Gloria was having labor pains. I hurried to our apartment and saw Gloria surrounded by several of the wives. One of the husbands was preparing to take her to the hospital. He said to me, "I'm glad to see you, for I have no idea where to take her."

A day after our arrival, I had checked out the hospital that was recommended by the doctor who we saw earlier in the day. We left Joey with one of the couples, and we took off for the hospital. I whipped into the front of the hospital and went up to the desk to check in only to find out that it was not the right hospital. They kindly told me the other hospital was near.

I checked Gloria in and found a comfortable waiting room. After a long night wait, the doctor suddenly showed up around five in the morning holding a beautiful baby girl. He said, "Here she is. Isn't she beautiful?"

Even though I was somewhat stunned by the sudden appearance of the doctor holding our new daughter, I quickly recovered to look upon one of the most beautiful babies I had ever seen. We had already picked out a girl and boy name. Her name would be Anne-Marie.

After a short time, Gloria was attending orientation classes with Anne-Marie in a carry-all. Joey was in the nursery. Orientation was a stimulating time. They prepared us in the best possible way for our adjusting to the field.

One thing stands out about the preparation in going to a mission on the field. The instructor said, "When you get to your new mission, you'll be warmly welcomed at first, but you'll not be a real part of the group. It'll take time. The missionary units in your mission have been through a lot of experiences together, and you'll be an outsider trying to come in to them. So, be patient and try to understand."

We later on found this to be true. It was not easy breaking into a Mission.

Getting On With the Going

After orientation, we went to Texas to spend a week with my parents before our departure for Vietnam. My Mom and Dad seemed to accept our going as part of our missionary calling. Mom told a friend, "I wish all my sons were missionaries."

Gloria's parents, Dewey and Stella Reece, were concerned about our going to Vietnam, but had accepted that we were going. Mrs. Stella had suggested that we might leave the children with her, but we said, "No, we're going as a family."

On the day of our departure from the Memphis airport, all of Gloria's family came to see us off. Perhaps they wondered if we would survive Vietnam. The news each day gave the death toll among our troops and each week it often was in the hundreds.

While Gloria was saying the last minute words of departure, I took Joey by the hand and headed for the airplane. I wanted to put our carry-ons in the overhead compartment. Since I was turning and waving and telling Joey to turn and wave, I only saw the boarding stairs in front of us. We walked up the stairs only to discover there was no plane attached to it. Embarrassed I tried to pass it off as an attempt to entertain my son.

Mrs. Stella saw my misadventure and said to Gloria, "I don't think you all are going to make it to Vietnam."

But we did in spite of a few glitches along the way. We were on a Pan Am flight, and dozens of soldiers were on the flight with us. We couldn't help but wonder how many of these soldiers would make it back home.

We planned two stops on the way to Saigon, Hawaii and Hong Kong. Ray and Lena Viliamu, friends from seminary days, were pastor and wife of a church in Hawaii. We planned on three days with them. Gloria's first cousin, Peggy Jean and family, also lived in Hawaii. Her husband was in the Navy.

Ray and Lena showed us around; we saw most of the tourist attractions. Our flight was scheduled to leave out on Monday morning at two o'clock. We told our hosts, "No need to see us off. Just get us to the airport."

After the evening service at Ray and Lena'a church, a couple came up to us and said, "Who's seeing you off at the airport?"

"Nobody. Our flight goes out at two in the morning. We don't expect anyone to see us off that time of the morning."

The couple said, "We'll be there to see you off. Somebody should be there to bid you God-speed."

Ray and Lena took us to the airport and stayed with us for thirty or forty minutes. After having prayer with us, they went home.

Just after midnight, I remembered what the couple had told us about seeing us off. "Gloria, you remember that couple who talked to us after the service? They said they were coming to the airport to pray with us before we leave. I wonder why they said that? I don't think I would want to see anyone off at two o'clock in the morning."

Just when I finished speaking, I looked up and saw the couple walking toward us, with their two –pre-teen-age children. The man said, "You know we served in Papua, New Guinea for several years, but we had to leave because I came down with sprue. I can't live in a climate like New Guinea. Now, we teach school at the Christian Academy here."

I was amazed at their coming at such a late hour. "You shouldn't have come. It's so late and you have school later on."

"We couldn't bear to see you all leave without someone seeing you off. We're night owls. We'll make it okay."

Through the years, I've never forgotten this family coming to the airport to bid us God-speed. I don't remember their names, but I still can visualize them coming toward us in the airport at Honolulu in June 1969. Their coming greatly encouraged us.

East is East

Rudyard Kipling got it right when he said, "Oh, East is East and West is West, and never shall the twain meet."

We arrived in Hong Kong and took a taxi to the downtown hotel that had been booked for us by the Foreign Mission Board. For two people who came from small town America, Hong Kong was overwhelming. The sidewalks were packed with hurrying crowds of people, while the taxis and other vehicles were bumper to bumper blowing their horns. Their driving on the left side of the street confused my mind and gave me a slight, dull headache.

Before we left Brownsville, several people told us to look up Dick and Ida Lusk who served with the Hong Kong Baptist Mission. To our pleasant surprise we found out that Dick and Ida lived near the Hong Kong Mission office. We introduced ourselves to them; so, began a friendship that has lasted through the years.

Missionaries from Asia had told us that the best place to buy cameras and other electronic goods was in Hong Kong. Charles Cowherd came to our hotel and introduced himself to us. He had served in China and left before the Communist took over. He told us that he knew all the best places for us to buy a super 8-movie camera and anything else along that line. He volunteered to take us to the stores.

Charles Cowherd enjoyed getting to know people. It was fun being with him. He had many experiences to share, and he did share many of them in such a winsome and humorous manner. Later on that afternoon he took us to the shops, and we bought everything that was on our list.

Carter Morgan, a seminary teacher, took us on a tour of the New Territories, located next to the China border. Carter drove around the curves with one hand, while he was pointing out the sights with another. Needless to say, it was hard to keep focused on what he was trying to point out to us. At one point, he said, "You're not looking."

Indeed, we were watching the curves and hoping that he would stay on the road.

When it came time to check out of our hotel, we didn't have enough money. We had misjudged the exchange rate. We called the Hong Kong Mission office and explained our problem. They said, "No problem. We'll pay for you and send the bill to the Vietnam Mission. You're not the first missionaries that we've bailed out."

We sent a telegram to the Vietnam Mission to tell them what time our plane was coming into Saigon. The Air Vietnam flight into Tan Son Nhut was to be our last leg of the trip; however, unbeknown to us, the plane that was to take us into Vietnam, was used in taking President Thieu to meet President Nixon on Midway Island.

We were booked on a Cathy Pacific flight that was to arrive four hours sooner than our regular flight; thus, when we arrived at Tan Son Nhut, no one met us. They were expecting us four hours later.

It was only eight o'clock in the morning, but it was already hot. To compound the difficulty of the situation, there was nothing to drink at the terminal. Trash from the night before, littered the area, so that Gloria felt anxious about letting little Joey run about.

To add to the difficulty of the situation, I did not have an address or phone number. Somehow this information got packed away in a suitcase or handbag. I couldn't locate it. I had so completely relied on the missionaries meeting us, that I had been sloppy in keeping up with the address and phone number of the mission office.

After thirty minutes of sitting and walking about the terminal, Gloria began to give me one of her "What are you going to do" looks. I needed to do something, but what could I do? I couldn't speak Vietnamese, and I didn't have any contact information.

A Vietnamese taxi driver followed me about the terminal saying every few minutes; "I take you where you want to go for cheap price, okay?"

Finally, I found a telephone and an old ragged phone book. Looking through the phone book, I found what I thought resembled the Baptist Mission. When I called the number, a woman answered in the Vietnamese language. I couldn't understand a word.

Frustrated, I thumbed through the phone book again and the only number and name that looked anything like the Baptist Mission was the number I had just called. I called it again and got the same woman and the same results.

"Where you want to go? I talk for you, okay?" said the persistent cab driver.

The taxi cab driver that followed me closer than a brother could talk on the phone for me. That's an idea. I motioned for the taxi man to stand ready to talk and I dialed the same number. He talked to the woman, and she told him it was the Baptist Mission office, and she would get a missionary on the line to talk with me.

I've never been so glad to hear an American voice, as the voice of Bob Davis, one of the Baptist Missionaries. He apologized for the mission not meeting us and said he would come out now to get us. I said, "No, we'll come on by taxi. You tell the taxi where to go. We're to dry and thirsty to wait another forty minutes."

When we arrived at the Mission office, the missionaries there more than made up for anyone not meeting. There gave us a warm welcome. We were taken to Jim and Margaret Gayle's house, which was located near the mission office. Margaret served us a large glass of tea, Texas style. The tea really refreshed us!

After visiting for a while, we were taken to the mission guest house to rest and spend the night. It was to be a memorable night.

Hello Vietnam!

The mission guest house was located behind the mission office. We were to stay there during our first days in Saigon. Before going to bed, we sat out in the court yard and watched the traffic go by. We were startled when we saw a gang of Vietnamese "Cowboys" flying down the street on their motorcycles, with the police chasing after them, shooting their guns in the air. Gloria turned to me and said, "Hey, it's like the wild, wild west."

That was our introduction to our first evening in Saigon. More was to come later on in the night. Around two o'clock in the morning, a huge explosion shook the guest house and jarred me out of my sleep. I staggered over to look out the window to the court yard. In my dazed and groggy condition, I could see several Viet Cong charging across the yard toward out apartment. Jarred out of my sleep, I took another look and saw that it was only shadows dancing in the pale moonlight.

After three days in Saigon, checking in with the Vietnamese government, we boarded a flight on Air Vietnam for Dalat, located in the Central Highlands. Dalat is a cool mountainous city that is a favorite tourist spot. It is known in Vietnam as the "Honeymoon City," because so many newly-weds go there for their honeymoon.

We studied the Vietnamese language in Dalat for the next eighteen months. One could call our time in Dalat our honeymoon years, for the two years spent in that beautiful city will forever be etched in our memory, as the best two years of our missionary experience.

Our first night, in our two-story, rented French-style house was traumatic. At two o'clock in the morning, the fury of war broke out in our back yard. Hand grenades were exploding in our yard, tracer bullets were whizzing past our bedroom window.

The hairs stood up on the back of my neck. Gloria and I ran into the children's bedroom, next to our room, picked them up and lay on the floor. They stirred a little, but never woke up.

The next morning, I asked our resident missionary, Sam Longbottom, if he had heard the shooting and explosions. He said, "No, I didn't hear anything. I slept through the night."

I didn't mention to Sam that the shoot-out took place in our back yard, for that would identify me as a new, uptight missionary focused on the war.

The veteran missionaries, who had been in Vietnam for a number of years, didn't want to talk about the war. When the missionaries met together, they talked about their work, family or something light and funny that had happened to them, or someone else. They had a studied indifference about the war situation that helped them to stay focused on their mission.

After being in Vietnam for several years, with the war in progress, I can understand why they tried to ignore the war. They focused on their mission in coming to Vietnam, getting out the Good News to the hearts of the Vietnamese people. The Vietnamese, at that time, were war-weary and longing for peace. The missionaries knew that only the Prince of Peace, Jesus, could bring them true peace.

We were in Dalat for eighteen months of language study. When we arrived in Dalat,

Joey was eighteen months old and Anne-Marie six months. We hired a Vietnamese woman to help with the house work and to keep the children, while we studied the Vietnamese language.

Mr. Ngoc came to our house four times a week to teach us how to hear and speak Vietnamese. He was proud of the Vietnamese language, and he held us to a strict course of study. He would say, "Tomorrow morning I expect you to know these words and be able to pronounce them clearly."

The next morning we were prepared, because we had to face our teacher.

Mr. Ngoc never let us get away with slurred, lazy pronunciation. Sometimes, we resented Mr. Ngoc coming down so hard on us, but a few years later we were thankful for his strict tutelage. The Vietnamese would often say to us, "Your pronunciation is so good and clear."

After a year of study in Dalat, we experienced the war in a real, close way.

Attack on Dalat

It was a beautiful Friday evening, and we had guests over for dinner. After a delicious meal, we adjourned to the living room to fellowship together and to share stories. A missionary couple, two single missionary ladies and a sergeant, from the military compound across town, made up the group.

We had such a wonderful time of sharing, laughing and feeling good about being together that our guests did not notice that it was a few minutes until curfew time. "Thanks, it was a terrific time. We've gotta get on the way fast," were the words hurriedly spoken, as the guests rushed out the door.

Sergeant Will Kurkendyle was depending on me to take him across town to his compound. I said to him, "Will, we'll never beat the curfew. How about spending the night and I'll take you to the compound early in the morning?"

"Okay, sounds good to me," Will said, "Is it safe in this part of town?"

"Yeah, it's quiet here. No problem."

Will slept on a sleeper downstairs. At two o'clock in the morning, we were shaken out of our sleep, by artillery, incoming mortar rounds hitting the National Police station, four hundred yards uphill from our house, and small arms fire. It sounded like the Battle of the Budge.

I looked out the window and saw tracer bullets streaking by our house. I could hear the thunder and roar of war coming from the direction of the Vietnamese

National Military Academy. Explosions and flares lit up the sky in that part of the city.

A barrage of mortar shells hit the police station. I said to Gloria, "We better get the kids and get downstairs; if they overshoot the police station, they may hit us."

Downstairs, Gloria and the children went under the stair case. I went over to Will who was sitting by the window holding his M-16. He looked tense, like a soldier about to go into battle. I tried some levity to loosen up the situation. "Will, like I said, it's a quiet neighborhood."

Will did not smile. He only gripped his M-16 tighter as he looked at me. He didn't say a word.

When the mortar barrage was over, we went back upstairs and attempted to get some sleep. Another barrage came slamming into the area thirty minutes later. Again, we rushed downstairs with the children. Will was still sitting by the window with his M-16.

After the second time of going downstairs, I said to Gloria, "I'm exhausted and I know you are also. No shells have come close to us. Let's commit it to the Lord and grab some sleep."

We did that and we were able to get several hours of sound sleep.

Around five o'clock, I was awakened by the sound of soldier boots pounding the pavement of the nearest street. Looking out the bedroom window, I saw a platoon of South Vietnamese soldiers carrying their weapons at port arms and double timing toward an orphanage located a quarter of a mile uphill from our house.

Later I learned that a contingent of Viet Cong soldiers had chased the Nuns and children out of the orphanage and had holed up there to make a fight out of their incursion into the city.

During the day we heard small arms fire and mortar rounds coming from the orphanage area. At two o'clock in the afternoon, a helicopter swirled over our house and shot its rockets at the orphanage. The explosion was deafening and shook our house.

Just after the rocket attack, a military vehicle from Will's compound drove up and picked him up. Will looked relieved to be back with his military buddies. The sergeant driving the jeep offered to take us to the compound for the night, but we politely declined. We thought that we'd be safer in our own house.

We were apprehensive about the coming night. The battle, up the hill from our house, had not been resolved. The fighting would be settled during the night hours. We really didn't know what was going to happen. But we knew that the military compound would be a more likely target.

Our next-door neighbor worked for USAID. While I was standing in my yard, he called out to me from his balcony. "Hey Joe, for heaven's sake don't shoot at anyone. It'll draw a lot of fire down on us."

"Don't worry about that. I'm not going to shoot anything."

He walked over to the side of the balcony nearer to me. "Joe, I've got hand grenades. If anyone tries to come up my stairs, they'll meet a grenade rolling down on them. Would you like a couple of them?"

"No thanks, we'll make it okay."

At midnight, we heard the battle break out. Automatic weapons, grenades with mortars chiming in, reverberated down the hill toward us. After twenty minutes the firing stopped and a silence pervaded the neighborhood.

We woke up to a beautiful and quiet Sunday morning, and wondered what had happened in the battle up the hill from us.

Our next-door neighbor came over at ten o'clock and told us what he had heard on his military radio. "All the firing that we heard was the ARVN Troops laying down a barrage of fire before they charged the Orphanage. When they got in the orphanage, they saw that the Viet Cong had all escaped. The Viet Cong dug fox holes in the back yard, and hid in them until the firing ceased, then they stealthily slipped away when the ARVN made a frontal assault."

"What happened on the other side of the city? I asked.

"A North Vietnamese unit tried to get into the academy, but they were beaten back by the students and their American Advisors. They killed sixteen NVA. The city is clear now. You can go downtown or wherever. You all have been in all weekend; I know you must want to move around."

"Yeah, we're ready to go somewhere. It's been a tense weekend."

I asked Gloria, "Where would you like to go?

"Let's go to the Christian Missionary Alliance Compound and see how the missionaries are doing there."

When we arrived at the compound, we were surprised at the response of the missionaries. They all rushed out to our car and asked numerous questions. "How did you all get here? What has happened in the city? Have any missionaries been captured or killed?"

The compound was located on the edge of the city and the missionaries were somewhat isolated from all that was going on. They had been listening to the Voice of Australia. The VOA had reported that Dalat had been captured by the Communist Forces. The missionaries were expecting, at any minute, to be captured by the North Vietnamese.

As the bearers of good news, we were given an extremely warm welcome.

Scouting out the Land

After finishing our allotted time of studying the language, we were assigned to Nha Trang as church planters. Having studied the Vietnamese language for a certain length of time did not mean we were fluent. It meant that we had nailed down the basics.

Gloria and I had the basics, and we had to build on what we had learned in our language study.

Now, the immediate task before us was to move to Nha Trang. Everyone who has moved their household goods to another location knows that moving is a hassle.

Before we moved, I had to go to Nha Trang and try to find us a suitable house. I arranged to fly to Nha Trang on an Australian Caribou. The small American airfield near Dalat was a suitable field for the Caribou which was built for short runways and unprepared landing strips.

Although it was a noisy ride, the Caribou landed me and two others safely on the Nha Trang Air Base. After landing, I grabbed my small bag and caught a ride into town at the gate.

Booking into a small hotel in downtown Nha Trang, I ate a lunch of fried rice at the hotel restaurant. While eating I decided that I would walk about the city and look for a house, rather than riding around in a taxi.

The balmy hot weather broke me out in a sweat, but I enjoyed walking around and relating to the local people. After spending a year-and-a-half in language study, I did know enough of the Vietnamese language to ask questions and to seek information.

I found out quickly that it was going to be difficult to find a house in Nha Trang. An American Army Base and Air Force Base were located in Nha Trang, along with some Green Berets, plus a Korean Army Base.

Besides all these military bases, there was a large group of American contractors and a good number of missionaries. Houses that were suitable for Westerners were scarce; however, I did find a house that looked suitable.

The neighbors told me, "An American missionary couple lives in the house, but they are gone on vacation now. They are going back to America."

There was a strange thing about the house. The couple's car was chained to the house. Later on, I found out why.

The neighbors said, "The landlord has a hardware store downtown. You can talk to him about renting the house."

The neighborhood was rather shabby looking and the car thing bothered me, but there was nothing else available. I went downtown and talked to the owner of the house. He was eager to rent the house to another American, so we made arrangements after a few minutes.

The other couple would be back in a week; therefore, we could move in two weeks. Having nailed down the house and the time, I went back to the Nha Trang Air Base and met the pilot of a small two-passenger plane going to Dalat. He was pleased to have me go with him and see his expertise as a pilot. He scared the life out of me!

The flight was pleasant, until we began circling to land at the small air strip. He said, "Hold on tight. We'll have to do the cork-screw to land on this small air strip."

I did hold on, and he did make an okay landing, but my head was spinning when we landed. Back with my feet on the ground, I had two weeks to get our household goods together for a move to Nha Trang.

A Memorable Moving Experience

The two weeks passed, and Gloria and I mapped out a moving plan. I would drive the VW van loaded with family valuables and memos, plus our dog Wolf. She would fly down later with Joey and Anne-Marie.

On the given morning, I loaded the van and with our dog, Wolf, set out for Nha Trang. The truck with our household goods preceded me. The plan was for me to follow him to our new house.

When we were about ten miles from Cam Ranh, my VW van went dead. It just quit; the engine would not even turn over. The truck with our household goods went sailing down the highway, seemingly unaware of my predicament.

Not only did I have car trouble, I had stomach trouble with a bad case of diarrhea. A pain struck me and I ran for the nearest grove of banana trees. After finding relief, I felt tired and washed-out. I sat down under a coconut tree and looked up at the lazy white clouds on a summer-like day. I thought of the days of growing up on a farm in Noonday, Texas, and sitting under the sweet gum tree beside the swimming hole and dreaming of going to far-away places.

A prayer formed in my heart. "Lord, I'm here because You called me to come here and serve this country with the Gospel of Christ. Now, I'm in trouble and I don't know what to do. Help me! I'm praying this prayer in Jesus name and for His honor and glory. Amen"

After my prayer, I walked back to the highway to check on the van. At the moment I stepped on the road, a vehicle drove up. A cherry voice said in Vietnamese

English, "Hey, you American. You have problem with your car?"

"Yes, I do. It quit running. I don't know what the problem is with it. Can you give me a ride into Cam Ranh?"

"Yeah, I can give you a ride. I live there and I'm going home now. Where do you want to go?"

"I have a friend who lives in Cam Ranh, Jim Gayle. He's a missionary. Do you know him?"

"Yeah, I know Mr. Gayle. Everybody knows him. I can take you to his house."

God does answer prayer! He took me to Jim's house. After explaining to Jim what had happened, he said, "Let's go and pull your car in to Cam Ranh and I'll put it in a trustworthy garage to get it fixed. You can take my van and go on to Nha Trang to get your truck unloaded."

Praise the Lord for Jim Gayle's generous and helpful heart. He, Margaret, and their three sons, Kyle, Kurt and Kent had served for six years in Vietnam. They had been faithful through many difficult and dangerous times. Later on, they served with us in Indonesia.

With Jim's newer car, I drove on to Nha Trang and to the newly rented house. The truck was waiting for me at the gate. The driver said, "What happened to you? When I looked in the mirror, you were not there. I never did see you again on the road."

I said, "My van broke down twenty miles from Cam Ranh. You were going so fast that you didn't see me. My friend in Cam Ranh loaned me his car."

The truck was loaded with some heavy pieces of furniture and appliances. How were we going to unload the heavy things? Then I remembered my fellow missionary, Sam Longbottom, in Dalat, using boards set at an angle from the truck bed, to slide heavy furniture and appliances down to the ground.

I went over to our neighbor and borrowed four two by six boards. In a short time, the driver and I had unloaded the truck, howbeit; all the household goods were in the yard. The driver was in a hurry and roared off in his truck. Since he had waited for me, at the house for several hours, I didn't ask him to help me put the goods in the house.

I stood for a few moments looking at my household goods, thinking: *Someone will steal all these things during the night, unless I keep an eye on it.*

Then I remembered my dog, Wolf. He could guard the goods. I went out to the van and let Wolf out. Was he ever happy to get out of the van. I put him in the spacious yard that had a fence around it with concertina wire a foot high on top of the fence. He raced happily about the yard.

It was around 5:pm and I had not had anything to drink or eat in hours. I was on the verge of dehydration. Going back inside the house, I was surprised, but pleased to see a telephone and some numbers of the ex-pat community. The SIL Center was one of the numbers. I called the number hoping to make contact with one of the Wycliffe missionaries.

One of the missionaries answered and I explained my dilemma to him. I said, "I just got here, and I haven't had any water for half a day, and I can't drink out of this faucet. Could you, or someone, bring over a gallon of water for me. I can't leave the house with all of my goods out in the yard."

Ken was the second missionary sent into my life that day to refresh me, so I could carry out my mission of moving. He said, "Yes, I'll be there in a few minutes."

Ken did arrive in a few minutes with two gallons of water and some sandwiches. I told him, "Ken, you've saved me. I couldn't have made it through the night without some water."

I guzzled down about a gallon of water in an hour's time. Feeling like I had a new lease on life, I began preparation for the night. Dead tired after a long and traumatic day, I knew I needed a good night's rest. But how about my goods? *I'll commit them to the Lord and commit Wolf to watching over them.*

With that thought in mind, I prayed and laid down on a blanket pallet. In about ten seconds I was sound asleep.

Awaking with a start, I noticed that daylight was breaking. What about my household goods? I jumped up and went out in the yard and was greeted by Wolf with a wagging tail. Everything looked intact. The household goods all needed to be in the house before another night fell.

Who could I get to help me? The missionaries helped me with water and sandwiches, but I couldn't call on them to help move things. They are busy people. The locals? No, I can't trust my goods to strangers. I'll do it myself. I'm strong and I can slide and wig waggle furniture and appliances into their proper place in the house. The house is all tile, so things will move easily on the floor.

With that thought in mind, I started moving the kitchen appliances first. I put a piece of cardboard under the fridge and stove and they slid easy enough on the tile floor. Then came the table and chairs. After that I found the boxes containing the eating and cooking utensils.

Next, I put up the beds in their respective rooms. I remembered the last thing Gloria told me before I left

Dalat. "Be sure," she said, "to set up the kitchen and bedrooms first. With those set up, we can start living. Later on, we can set up other rooms in the house."

Gloria and the children were to arrive at 11:30am. At 10:30am I had the house as ready as possible. I finished off the last of my water and went to a nearby kiosk and bought me a can of coke. Drinking all of it, I felt a burst of energy.

I arrived at the airport several minutes before the Air Vietnam flight landed from Dalat. Although it had been only two days since I had seen them, it had seemed like an eternity. So many things had happened. I hugged and kissed them like I had been gone a year.

It was a lot of fun showing Gloria our new house. She seemed pleased with how spacious the yards were and how open and light the rooms were in the house. There was a patio that separated the main part of the house from the kitchen. The patio could be used in various ways.

Now we were set up in our new house and ready to begin a new ministry.

A Lesson Learned

Several weeks after moving into our new house, we had our VW van back from the garage in Cam Ranh, and I had returned Jim Gayle's van to him. One morning, I planned on driving to downtown Nha Trang to pick up some nails and other things from the hardware store.

But once again our van would not start. I had also planned on taking the family out for lunch at a popular French restaurant, but it seemed like that family outing was going to be delayed or cancelled.

Then it occurred to me that we could get two cyclos to take us to the restaurant. The Vietnamese Cyclos were much like the Chinese pedicab. The driver of the Vietnamese cyclo sat behind the passenger and pedaled the two wheel cab forward.

At lunch time, I went out on the street and called for two cyclos to come to our house to pick us up as a family. Gloria and one child would go in one cyclo, and I would take the other child in the cyclo with me.

I bargained with the cyclo drivers, and they agreed to take us to the restaurant for seventy-five Dong. Since I prided myself on my bargaining ability, I felt good about the price.

We arrived at the restaurant in a happy mood and had a delicious meal. When we had finished eating lunch, I told Gloria, "You and the children wait here in front of the restaurant and I'll go out and get us two cyclos."

Two cyclos pedaled up to me, after I had walked only fifteen yards from Gloria and the children. The drivers motioned for me to get in. I climbed in one of the cyclos and pointed to my family. The two cyclos wheeled over to pick up Gloria and the children.

At that point of time, I began to bargain with the drivers about the price. They wanted one hundred and seventy-five Dong. "No," I said, "We came here for seventy-five Dong. I'll pay no more than a hundred Dong."

"No," they shouted, "We want one hundred seventy five Dong."

"I won't pay that much," I said, "I'll get us two other cyclos."

When we climbed out of the cyclos, the drivers said, "You owe us one hundred Dong for riding in our cyclos."

"We rode for five meters in your cyclos. We don't need to pay for that. Besides, we were in the process of bargaining with you. You go get another customer, and we'll get us two other cyclos."

I stepped away from the two cyclos and walked down the street to get two other cyclos. Hearing the crunch of gravel behind me, I turned to see the two cyclo drivers running toward me with their fists cocked. I had no choice but to defend myself. I clobbered both of them, and they hastily backed off.

Then a strange happening took place. Dozens of cyclo drivers who were resting in the shade, or were sleeping in their cyclos, began to line up some ten yards in front of me. They begin to pick up rocks, and a few of them held lead pipes.

Realizing the gravity of the situation, I yelled to Gloria, "You all go back to the restaurant. If you see some ex-pats tell them to come and help out. I think I can outrun these guys for a while. Love you. Go now."

The line of about ten cyclo drivers moved toward me. I turned and ran at a fast pace. I praise the Lord that I was in great shape, and I could run fast. Getting a great start on the cyclo drivers, I jumped out about thirty yards ahead of them. Some of them threw rocks at me, but they fell woefully short.

Seeing that I was outrunning them, several of the cyclo drivers enlisted motorcycle drivers to carry them in the chase to catch me. This was a potentially dangerous situation, for the cyclo drivers sitting behind the motorcycle drivers had large rocks and purposed to nail me as the motorcycle passed me.

Seizing up the situation, I ran along like I didn't see the motorcycle, and the rock thrower. When the motorcycle was even with me, I suddenly stopped and the rock whizzed by me, missing me by two or three feet. After the third attempt to bean me with a rock from the back of a motorcycle, I saw a van full of Americans coming down the street to rescue me.

The Americans were spoiling for a fight and each one had a lead pipe. I saw that it could lead to a serious encounter. I said to them, "Hey, I'm okay. There was just a misunderstanding between myself and a cyclo driver. Let's not have a problem with them."

The Americans took me back to the restaurant to meet Gloria and the children. Then they took us home. "Thanks," I told them. "I appreciate you coming to my rescue. It got a little touchy there."

Several months later, I led a cyclo driver to receive Christ in his life as Lord and Savior. Through him we led other cyclo drivers to confess Jesus as Savior and to follow Him as Lord. Eventually, I became acquainted with all of the cyclo drivers in Nha Trang. Some of them remembered the day they chased me. They looked at me with an embarrassed grin on their face.

Oh yea, about the lesson I learned. Life is more valuable than one hundred Dong. I learned that Americans are expected to pay more, and we can pay more than Nationals.

There are three tiers of prices in most third world countries. First is the price for the National, which will be the lowest. Secondly, there is the price for the missionary or foreigner who speaks the local language. Thirdly, there is the price for the American or other foreigners.

I'm willing to pay the highest price and, also, give a tip. After all, we have so much and they have so little. Yes, I learned my lesson.

A Reluctant Preacher

When we arrived in Nha Trang, we didn't know anyone. The first Sunday was coming upon us, and we planned to attend the small Baptist Church located in the Phouc Hai area. Saturday afternoon a group of leaders from the church visited us. They welcomed us, and then they informed me that I would preach tomorrow, Sunday morning.

"Preach tomorrow!" I exclaimed, "I just finished language school, and I'm not ready to preach."

The group stood up to leave, and the leader, with a note of finality in his voice, said, "You will preach tomorrow."

The churches representatives exited the door and left me dazed. "I can't believe this." I said to Gloria.

"You better believe it and get on your sermon."

"They think I can speak Vietnamese like Walter Routh or Jim Gayle. Those guys have been here for seven and eight years."

Gloria walked over and put her hand on my shoulder. "You're all they have now. You don't have a choice, and the church will be looking for you tomorrow morning. You can do it."

I shifted into my emergency gear and headed for my office. In a few more hours I would be standing before a Vietnamese congregation trying to communicate the gospel to them, in their own language. That was an impossible assignment that's only possible with the Lord's anointing help.

I spent as much time in prayer, as I did studying for my sermon. Sunday School started at eight and the worship hour at nine. We were expected to be there for the opening Bible study period at eight. Needless to say, I burned the midnight oil.

While waiting to be introduced to the pulpit, I whispered a prayer, "Here goes Lord. I will give it my best. You will have to do the rest. Just take my inadequate language and use it for Your Glory."

I must say when I stood up to deliver my sermon; every eye and ear was riveted on me. They were taking stock of me, looking me over. What kind of missionary do we have here? Can he really preach in our language?

When I finished, I could tell by the looks on the faces of the people that my sermon was not communicated very well. After a few moments of silence, this fact was verified by Ba Chau (Mrs. Chau). She stood up and said, "Missionary, why can't you speak Vietnamese like Mr. Routh and Mr. Gayle?"

I didn't expect a broadside like that. After all, I told them that I didn't want to preach, for I wasn't ready. I had given my best effort, and for that I was humiliated. Standing before the congregation dazed, I mumbled, "Pray for me."

The leaders told me after church that I was their pastor and preacher, for they had no one else. I was it! Like it or not.

That week I studied every day and spent hours trying to get my manuscript in order. Gloria listened to my pronunciation and corrected me on a number of words.

One of the problems I faced with this congregation was that the majority of them came from Quang Ngai Province where they spoke Vietnamese in their own distinct way. You might compare it to the Brooklyn accent in American English. Evidently, Walter

Routh and Jim Gayle had adjusted their Vietnamese language to the Quang Ngai accent.

Gloria and I had studied Vietnamese with Mr. Ngoc who was a highly educated teacher from Central Vietnam. Now, I had to preach again, and I could only use the Vietnamese that I had studied, the Central Vietnamese accent.

Once again, I stood before the congregation and shared my message. And once again, Ba Chau stood up. She said, “Missionary, we can’t understand you.” I felt a surge of anger, but I simply said, “Pray for me.”

For the second straight week, I studied a number of hours and practiced my pronunciation. I knew I had to face the church and Ba Chau on Sunday morning. After I finished my third sermon, I stood and waited. Ba Chau did not stand up! Praise the Lord!

Ba Chau did more for my Vietnamese language than anyone else. Later on, as the weeks and months went by, Ba Chau became one of our favorites in the church.

When we returned to Vietnam in 1999, after been evacuated out in 1975, we returned to Nha Trang and went by to see Ba Chau. She was in her late eighties. Her daughter said, “Me (mother) said she would see the missionary before she dies. Now her prayer is answered.”

A Prayer Answered

After getting settled in, I began to go out to the streets and markets to meet people and to share the Good News of Jesus when I had the opportunity. Going out alone, in the Vietnamese culture was no fun. Often, I was misunderstood.

The fact is, I needed a Vietnamese counterpart. The American military had their counterparts, and I began to realize that I needed someone to go with me. A Vietnamese counterpart could help me deepen my language, interpret situations, and deflect some of the harshness sometimes directed toward me.

Having settled in my mind that I wanted and needed someone to go with me, we begin to pray for someone. The Lord would have to send someone. There was no one in the church. Most of the males in the church were old men or early teenage boys. The majority of the able- bodied men were in the military. I could not think of anyone. Gloria and I begin to pray for someone to work with me.

One afternoon, two months after we began praying for a counterpart, someone came banging on our gate at 12:30pm. It is a habit, and a custom, for everyone to take a short rest between twelve and one o'clock. It's a sacred time. You don't visit anyone or disturb anyone during that one hour break.

Hearing the banging on our gate, I said to Gloria, "Who is banging on our gate at this time? Don't they know that we're resting?"

I went out to see who had the audacity to come to our gate during the rest period. A young Vietnamese man, in air force dungarees, was standing outside the gate. He said, "Are you the missionary who's goes out witnessing about Jesus?"

"Yes, I am."

"Can I go with you?"

"Yes, you can. Come in!"

Leading the way for the young man, I saw Gloria peeping from the window. I confirmed answered prayer, "Gloria, our prayers have been answered."

The young man was Long (Lum) Pham. Long served in the Vietnam Air Force as an air controller at the Nha Trang Air Base. He said, "I'm off every Tuesday and Sunday. I can help you share the Gospel. I am a member of the Grace Baptist Church in Saigon."

That day began a fruitful year and a half of working with Long Pham, in getting out the Gospel of Christ in Nha Trang. The first thing we did on Sunday afternoon was to visit our members. Some of them had not attended worship services in months. Other members who did come to church needed to be encouraged.

The second week on Tuesday, we began to visit church prospects. There were a number of people who had visited our worship services. Our visitation resulted in an increased attendance. The church began to grow.

A large group of high school students lived in the Phuoc Hai neighborhood. Two of the students, brothers, Tien and Hien, attended our services. Hien played the organ and five other musical instruments. Working with Tien and Hien, we began to touch other high school students with the Gospel of Christ. Soon we had a good core group of young people who attended our worship services.

Let the Islands Know

One day Long said to me, "There's an island off the coast of Nha Trang that has a population of 1500 people. Most of them are fishermen. I feel strongly the Lord wants us to go there with the Gospel."

"How about next Tuesday? I asked, "How are we going to get there?"

Long said, "We can rent a fishing boat. There are many boats at Cau Da, the dock where the fishing boats come and go."

The next Tuesday we rented a fishing boat. When you rent a boat in Vietnam, the owner, or an assigned person, goes with you to steer the boat.

When we arrived at the island, I was in for a big shock. I thought that we would be warmly received. On the contrary, a group of young people, 12 to 14 years of age, spotted me as a foreigner and decided to to give me a warm welcome; but not the kind I expected. They began to throw rocks at us. Long and I did a fast trot, with the rock-throwing young people in pursuit. We came to a neat looking little cottage that had two coconut trees in the yard.

To get away from the zinging rocks, we ducked behind the coconut trees. The owner of the house, seeing what was happening, came outside and so verbally chastised the young people that they left in a hurry.

The man invited us into his house. He said, "My name is Tuan and I am the village tailor. What are your names and what are you doing here?"

We told him our names and said, "We have come to share the Good News of Jesus Christ with the island of Hon Tre."

Tuan said, "I have heard something about Christ, but I have never understood. Can you help me understand more clearly this Gospel of Christ?"

After giving an affirmative answer, we explained the Good News of Jesus with Tuan for the next 45 minutes. Tuan was eager and ready to know about Jesus and eternal life.

When Long asked him was he ready and willing to commit his life to the Lordship of Christ, he said, "I am ready, for I've been waiting for a long time to know about Jesus and eternal life. I want to give my life to Jesus now, and I want to serve Him."

After we prayed with Tuan, we asked him, "Would you like for us to come every Tuesday to study the Bible with you and your friends?"

"Yes," he said, "I want you to come. I have many friends on this island and they will come if I invite them."

Every Tuesday, Long and I rented a boat and went to teach a Bible study at Tuan's house. His house was usually full of people. As the months went by, we added new believers to the group.

After we had ten new believers, along with Tuan, we had a baptism service in the South China Sea. The new believers were organized into a church.

In 1999, Gloria and I returned to Nha Trang, along with our oldest son, Joey, and his wife, Stephanie. We visited the Phouc Hai Church and members that we knew who were still in Nha Trang.

On the third day in Nha Trang, I said to Joey, "While Gloria and Stephanie are shopping, let's go to the island and visit Tuan and the church members."

We rented a fishing boat at Cau Da. Along with the owner, we motored out to Hon Tre Island. It had been twenty-four years since I had been to the island. On the way to the island, questions kept popping into my mind: Is Tuan still alive? Is the church still meeting?

After pulling into the dock, I started asking people, "*Ong Tuan, o dau*?" Where does Tuan live? No one seemed to know. I felt frustrated. Finally, the owner of the boat who accompanied us, said, "Let's go see the village chief and he will tell us where Tuan lives."

I did not want to go to the village chief, because I knew that he was a Communist Cadre. All village chiefs were members of the Communist Party; however, there seemed to be no other option, if I wanted to find Tuan. I said to the boat owner, "Yes, let's go see the village chief."

The village chief already knew about our presence, and he greeted us warmly. After serving us hot tea and chips, he said, "Tell me about America. I'm interested in your country."

For the next twenty minutes, I answered the village chief's questions about America. It turned out to be a pleasant time. At the end of the question and answer period, he said to me, "I like you. Tell me who you are looking for?"

I said, "Tuan the tailor."

The village chief smiled broadly. He said, "Everybody knows him. Just go outside and anyone can take you to his house."

When we went outside the chief's house, a crowd of people were waiting to take us to Tuan's house. They all knew where Tuan lived, but they were waiting for the village chief to give his approval before they would tell us where he lived.

A little lady with a conical straw hat led us, with thirty or forty people following, to Tuan's house. She knocked on Tuan's door and turned back to look at us with a big smile on her face. When Tuan opened the door, she said, pointing toward me, "Do you know who this is?"

Tuan, said, without changing expressions, "He's the missionary."

Tuan invited us into his house. The first thing that I saw upon entering was the Bible that I had given to him some twenty years ago. On his wall was a cross. Then I knew that the church was alive and doing well.

It was a festive-like occasion. Tuan sent some young people to get drinks and finger foods. We shared with one another about our lives in the past years. I asked Tuan, "How many believers are on the island?"

He looked around at the crowd of people looking in the windows and door, and leaned over toward me saying in a whisper, "Many, there are many."

Tuan escorted us back to our boat. He stood on the beach watching us until we were out of sight. I knew that I would probably never see him again this side of heaven.

Lifting my face upward, I felt the wet ocean spray on my face. Looking up I whispered a prayer of thanks for Tuan, and the day I had the privilege of meeting him. As the boat plowed the waves toward the Cau Da landing port, I thought about my last days in Vietnam in 1975.

The Last Days of the War

Soon after the last contingent of American troops left Vietnam on March 29, 1973, the country became more insecure. In May of that year, fellow missionary, Jim Kellam, and I were invited to go to Tuy Hoa to introduce a village to the Gospel of Christ. On the way, we fell in behind a South Vietnamese Army convoy consisting of twenty-five trucks.

We felt secure about tagging along with the convoy, until we reached a mountain pass. We were jarred out of our secure feelings, by bursts of fire from automatic rifles and hand grenades exploding. The first three trucks were ambushed by the Viet Cong. A fire fight ensured, as the South Vietnamese soldiers fought off the attackers and chased them up the mountain.

From that day on, we knew that we were going to be limited in our travel about the country.

The commanding officer of intelligence over Khanh Hoa Province, Captain Thong, was a good friend who often attended our church. He, and his wife Brenda, had dinner with us one evening, in February 1975. When Gloria and Brenda had retired to another room. Captain Thong and I talked about the war situation.

Captain Thong asked, "Joe, do you have a map of Vietnam?"

After I produced a map, he proceeded to show me where the North Vietnamese Army was located, and how imminent the threat was to South Vietnam. He said, with emotion, "Joe, if I were you, I would take my family out of Vietnam. The North Vietnamese can close down Tan Son Nhut Air Base any time they want too. They have captured Phouc Long District and are posed to attack Saigon when the time is right for them."

I was surprised at his assessment of the war, and that the condition of South Vietnam was much worse than I had imagined. He saw the stunned look on my face, and said, "Listen, when the situation becomes dangerous for you and your family, I'll send Brenda to warn you to leave."

Captain Thong's warning became more real on the first week in March. The North Vietnamese Army attacked the city of Ban Me Thuoc. The city was attacked so quick and vicious that it fell within a few hours. The fall of Ban Me Thuoc sent waves of fear throughout South Vietnam.

Soon after the fall of Ban Me Thuoc, Pleiku and Kontum fell two weeks later on March 17. Thousands of soldiers and civilians attempted to flee to the coast. Thirty thousand refugees were placed in a tent camp two miles north of Nha Trang. Gloria and I worked with our church to bring thirty fifty pound sacks of rice to the refugee camp.

The fall of South Vietnam came quicker than we could have imagined. We were getting ready to go to church on the last Sunday in March 1975, when we heard a banging at our gate. It was Brenda, Captain Thong's wife. She said, "I don't have time to come in. Thong says that the North Vietnamese Army has broken through the pass and are heading down Highway One. You need to get out, as soon as possible."

I said to Gloria, "You get our bags packed, and I'll check with the consulate about flights to Saigon."

When I arrived at the American Consulate, I could see no one except the Marine guard and a secretary. The secretary said, "The Consul is here. Just go right in."

Entering the Consul's office, I saw an unshaven man in a wrinkled suit and blood-shot eyes. It was obvious that he had been up all night. I asked, "How is it?"

"It's bad. We need to get all of you out as soon as we can. Come back tomorrow morning, and we'll have a time for your evacuation."

The next morning I arrived at the consulate before eight o'clock. A crowd of Americans and their Vietnamese wives were already there clamoring to get evacuated out of Nha Trang, before the North Vietnamese Army marched into the city. I caught the attention of the lady in charge of the evacuation and said to her, "I'm from the Baptist Mission. Yesterday the Consul told me to come back this morning to arrange for a time of evacuation."

I was totally surprised by the lady's response. She said, "The Vietnamese dependents are to be evacuated first. Then we'll arrange for you all to go out."

"Lady," I said, "the situation is dangerous and the American Consulate has a responsibility to get Americans out, especially our wives and children."

The lady put her hand on my arm. "Yeah, I know. You come back this afternoon and I'll arrange a flight for your wives and children tomorrow morning, okay? You men can go out later."

The flight for the missionary wives and children was at 10:30 the next morning. We men were a sad group as we watched the Air America DC-3 taxi down the runway with our families. We wondered if we would ever see them again. Would there be time for us to get out before the North Vietnamese Army came charging in?

When I drove back through town to our house, I saw that all offices and businesses were closed and boarded up. Deserted soldiers roamed the streets carrying their M-

16s. Robbing and vandalizing was already taking place, and there was a breakdown of law and order. Nha Trang was a dangerous city to be in.

Gloria had taken the small suitcase that was allowed. Its content was mostly memos with a change of clothes for each one of us. Everything else that we had accumulated over the past six years was left behind, including my library.

Coming back to our house, I felt the emptiness. No Gloria to greet me, and no voices of the children to warm my heart.

After a drink of cool water, I walked the three blocks to downtown, where the landlord owned a hardware shop. I needed to pay the landlord for a few month's rent, in case the South Vietnamese held off the invading Communist Army.

The landlord wanted a year's rent, in which I refused to pay. He said, "Our cowboys are holding them off and winning some battles."

While he was talking, one of his helpers came in and informed him that there were no tickets available on Air Vietnam. The landlord lost his composure and began to walk around in circles saying, "What are we going to do? What are we going to do?"

I left his question unanswered and walked back to my house. On the way I met a North Vietnamese acquaintance who had come South some twenty years before. He was a marked man on the North Vietnamese list. He knelt down weeping and pleading, "Take me with you please. They will kill me. Take me with you to America!"

I felt sorry for the man, and I wished that I could help him, but it was not in my power to help him, or the thousands of others who would like to escape out of

Vietnam. I spoke to him as casual as I could. "I'm not going to America. I'm going to my house now."

He stood up. "You are going to your house?"

The fear seemed to leave him, and he was normal. He said to himself as he walked away. "He's going to his house. Everything is okay."

I went back to my empty house, but events were going to change my situation in a very short time.

Not the Last Man out

While walking back to my house, I remembered what I had promised Gloria. I told her, "We'll not wait until the last minute to leave Saigon."

Now, I was concerned about getting out of Nha Trang before the North Vietnamese arrived. When I came to my house, a committee of South Vietnamese Baptist from Cam Ranh, were waiting for me. They wanted me to go to Saigon to get money to buy food for the thousands of Vietnamese fleeing from DaNang and the north area. Baptist World Alliance had sent thousands of dollars to help out in the crisis.

I agreed to go and left for the American Consulate to book a flight. An official told me that I could go on the one o'clock flight to Saigon, but if I came back, they could not guarantee me another seat. I told the official, "Put me down for the flight."

I boarded the one o'clock flight for Saigon. The driver of the bus who took us from the Consul to the to the Air America plane told us, "Get off the bus and get on the plane as quick as possible. There are people who will try to force themselves on the flight."

Ken Goad, the Baptist Mission Business Manager, met me at the airport in Saigon. He was so calm and relaxed, and I, on the contrary, was tense and stressed. I had just come from a city in chaos, where law and order had broken down.

As we drove through the city of Saigon, I could see why Ken was so calm. The city was calm, living in a false security. South Vietnamese troops cordoned off the city some forty miles. The chaos and confusion that characterized the cities north of Saigon was not yet in

Saigon; therefore, the population was going about their lives with business as usual.

On Friday, Danang was on verge of falling to North Vietnamese forces. No flights to Nha Trang, because all planes were in use to get people out of Danang before the Communist forces took control of the city. Saturday morning empty planes were going to Nha Trang, in an attempt to evacuate key military and government personal.

I headed out to catch a flight to Nha Trang, Bob Davis, a missonary friend, advised me not to return to Nha Trang. He said, "The city is about to fall. You don't want to be caught in that situation. You notice that all the planes going to Nha Trang are empty."

On Monday morning, my family and I boarded a flight to Manila. Several weeks later, the newspapers over the world headlined a picture of a North Vietnamese tank plowing through the gate of the Presidential Palace in Saigon. South Vietnam had fallen.

The door closed on our time to live and serve in Vietnam, but other doors opened for us to live and serve Christ Jesus in four other countries: Philippines, Indonesia, Zambia and Slovakia. Our third child, Elizabeth Gayle, was born in the Philippines, and our youngest, John Mark, was born in Indonesia.

The time of sharing the Gospel of Christ with other countries of the world was a wonderful and exciting time. If we could, we would do it again.

Someday in heaven, if I do receive a "Rusty Old Halo," I'll lay it at the feet of Jesus.

Papa Turman

Mam Turman

12 Year-old Joe

16-year-old Joe with his Mustang pony

High school half back

Joe with siters Bette, and Gayle and brothers Nick, Larry and Bud

Just out of Marine bootcamp

Running back for the Marines

College days

Joe and Gloria graduate from Southwestern Seminary

Joe and Joey and Dalat, Vietnam

Joe and family in Temanggung, Indonesia

Joey looking at Sgt. York's bronzed statue in Nashville

Joe and all the family in Israel